THE BEST

THE BEST ENGLISH, completed shortly before
Vallins's death, is the last of a notable trio of
books by this distinguished philologist—the
other two being GOOD ENGLISH and BETTER ENG-
LISH—on the nature, practice and problems of
written English. It deals at length with many of
the finer points of the subject, among them
Vocabulary, Style, and Speech in Literature,
and shows the same good taste, good sense and
lucidity, as the rest of Mr. Vallins's work in this
Field. His three inter-related books are essential
works for all who are interested in writing good
English. Each volume contains reading lists that
are valuable guides to the topics discussed.

By the same author in PAN Books:

GOOD ENGLISH

BETTER ENGLISH

THE BEST ENGLISH

G. H. VALLINS

PAN BOOKS LTD : LONDON

First published 1960 by Andre Deutsch Ltd.
This edition published 1963 by Pan Books Ltd.,
33 Tothill Street, London S.W.1

330 13007 2

2nd Printing 1964
3rd Printing 1970

Printed in Great Britain by Richard Clay (The Chaucer Press), Ltd.,
Bungay, Suffolk

CONTENTS

PREFACE

IN this book I have tried to remind the reader of certain techniques of composition – syntactical, idiomatic, rhythmical – he is bound to encounter in that kind of writing which we call literature, whether prose or verse. I have not essayed literary criticism in the ordinary sense, though of necessity it crops up here and there. Now and then, especially in my references to modern or 'modernist' literature, I have been provocative. For example, my chapter on Rhythm in Prose and Verse, in which I deliberately avoid the technicalities of Saintsbury and suggest that Hopkins's complicated account of his own 'sprung' rhythm (from which so much has developed in recent years) is a 'much ado about nothing', may seem an over-simplification to some, and merely perverse to others. However, there it is: I have at least tried to show that rhythm even in conventional verse is not a mere matter of iambs and anapaests vaguely related to the corresponding quantitative feet in the Classical languages; and that all rhythm, in prose and verse, has a kinship with the natural flow of ordinary speech, though this kinship is, as I think, exaggerated in, for example, the stream-of-consciousness technique, and in the more extreme experiments in modern poetry.

For the reader's convenience, I have, at the end, made a list of the chief books of reference and criticism mentioned in the text, together with a few others which he may find useful. Once again, I acknowledge with gratitude my debt to the Editor of the Language Library, Mr Eric Partridge, first for the stimulus and inspiration of his own books, and second for his encouragement and help in the preparation of this book of mine; and to my original publishers, Andre Deutsch Ltd, for their unfailing kindness and courtesy.

CHAPTER I

USAGE

THIS BOOK is, in the main, a study of memorable writing in prose and verse – the kind of writing which is commonly termed literature. It is not in the ordinary sense literary criticism, for the emphasis is on form and technique, on the construction of sentences, the choice of words, and the use of language generally. Not that (as is shown in later chapters) outward form can be separated from inward spirit. In memorable writing manner and matter are one; the prose (or verse) is, like the City of Jerusalem, at unity in itself. The inward spirit, indeed, defies analysis. But since the writer is bound by certain principles of language which he can neither escape nor ignore, the externals can in some measure be isolated, assessed, and criticized. Beyond the externals this book does not profess to go; it is a study of the inter-relationship of literature and linguistic usage.

To begin with, then, literature suggests and indeed implies the written word. It is true that it may have its immediate origin in speech, as for example an old ballad like *Chevy Chase*, or an oration of Burke or Bright. But once the memorable spoken word, whether in verse or prose, takes upon itself the permanence of ink, once it moves from the realm of hearing to the realm of seeing, it becomes 'literature', the proper arrangement (to come back to ultimate meanings) of *litterae*, the letters of the alphabet. But here, straightway, we come face to face with a basic question: What is the relationship of the spoken to the written language? It is a question that crops up from time to time in the succeeding chapters; and to it there is no single or easy answer. All that need be said here may be summed up in a parable or simile. There may be and often is between the two – spoken and written – a wide and obvious gap. We are aware of this in our own experience. The syntax and idiom of the voice, in common conversation, are not the syntax and idiom of the pen. Indeed, the spoken often tends to looseness and vulgarity while the written, for fear of catching the plague, becomes literary (in the wrong sense) and formal. But when the gap is narrowed, and the two are divided by only the merest fraction, there may occur at least one manifestation of literature. The spark jumps, as it were, between the points. 'When I am reading a book, whether wise or silly,' says Swift, 'it seems to me to be alive and talking to me.' It is an odd idea that a book should be actively talking rather than passively read; but for both writer and reader it is full of significance.

Since the term 'best English' is thus equated with literature, our approach must be historical; for what is memorably written defies (at least within our brief and finite reckoning) the onset of Time. Our English literature spans a period of well over a thousand years.

Swā clǣne hio wæs oðfeallanu on Angelcynne ðætte swīðe fēawe wǣron behionan Humbre þe hiora ðēnunga cūðen understandan on Englisc oððe furðum ān ǣrendge-wit of Lǣdene on Englisc āreccan, ond ic wēne ðætte nāūht monige begeondan Humbre nǣren.

It is King Alfred writing in one of the finest passages of our earliest prose; but anyone unacquainted with the element of Old English could do no more than recognize an odd word here and there. This is only saying, by way of extreme example, that the best English marches with the development of the language. The modernized version[1] (given below in a footnote) of King Alfred's sentence makes this plain enough. Obviously, the word order is different from ours. There are

---

[1] From the Preface to Alfred's Translation of Gregory's *Cura Pastoralis*. Literal rendering: 'So cleanly (= completely) it (i.e. learning) was fallen away in England that very few [there] were on this side of Humber who their mass-book could understand in English or even a letter from Latin into English translate, and I think that not many beyond Humber [there] were not.'

also one or two differences of idiom: Alfred procures his
emphasis, for example, by a clear and resounding double
negative – '*not* many were *not*'. Less obviously, his vocabulary consists only of what we now call native words: it cannot draw upon the vast riches of derivatives that came into
English after his time. Moreover, in the original several
words have inflected forms that have long since disappeared.
In brief, the best English of eleven hundred years ago and
that of today are (or seem to be) poles apart. They are, in
fact, two different manifestations – one at the beginning and
one at the end – of the essential continuity of the living
language, a continuity that is traceable in the written (or
printed) word.

This progress, the change in vocabulary, syntax, and
idiom, is obvious enough when we compare the language of
King Alfred with the language of Queen Elizabeth II. It is
not quite so obvious when the comparison is made within the
limits of what may be loosely called modern English, beginning, say, a little before the reign of the first Elizabeth.
By that time inflections had disappeared except the few that
now remain. Because of some differences of spelling the
language appears a little strange to the modern eye; but that
is all. It is comprehensible without the aid of glossary and
grammar book:

> Now, of versifying there are two sorts, the one Auncient,
> the other Moderne: the Auncient marked the quantitie of
> each silable, and according to that, framed his verse: the
> Moderne, observing onely number (with some regarde of
> the accent), the chiefe life of it standeth in that lyke sound-
> ing of the words, which wee call Ryme. Whether of these
> be the most excellent, would beare many speeches. The
> Auncient (no doubt) more fit for Musick, both words and
> tune observing quantity, and more fit lively to expresse
> divers passions, by the low and lofty sounde of the well-
> weyed silable.

When we read that (it is from Sir Philip Sidney's *Apologie for
Poetrie*, 1595), we are conscious of a different texture and

pattern. But the meaning is not obscured; the language is recognizably our own. Nevertheless, we cannot apply to it the tests of modern grammar and usage. The custom of language changes like the custom of life; changes, indeed, with it, reflecting (however faintly) the differences in the succeeding generations. It is not necessary to go back nearly four hundred years to Sidney. Any two authors separated by no more than twenty or thirty years are not using precisely the same language. Some changes will have occurred even in so brief a time – imperceptibly, probably, in accidence and syntax but reasonably plain in vocabulary and idiom. Though the 'best English' is in a sense timeless, any judgement of it cannot be separated from the element of Time.

Yet that is, in some measure, an over simplification. 'The present,' says Landor, in a notable and beautiful passage, 'like a note in music, is nothing but as it appertains to what is past and what is to come.' That is as true of language as it is of all other human affairs. Speech cannot, of course, detach itself from the past, but it leans, on the whole, towards the present and the future; it gathers the harvest of the latest changes, and with words and phrases 'fire-new from the mint' anticipates those that are still to be. This is only to say that the 'livingness' of language is most clearly manifested in speech, which welcomes, assimilates, experiments, leaving the ultimate rejection or acceptance to the permanence of writing. But the written language tends to look backwards; or, to put it another way, its onward progress is slower, since the writer is accustomed to weigh novelty against tradition, to exclude the informal or colloquial in favour of the formal or literary.[1] This is true of that ordinary English in which we communicate with one another. We never (or rarely) express ourselves in a letter as we do in conversation, either face to face or on the telephone. We try to marshal our words and give shape to our sentences: to forget colloquialism and remember grammar. As for business and official English, that is notoriously formalized. It retains constructions,

[1] Throughout this book the term *literary* as an epithet for *language* is used as a convenient, though not satisfactory, antonym of *colloquial*.

phrases, words, which have by long use become (in Shakespeare's phrase) overworn, and survive only in a kind of
living death. The history of officialese or gobbledygook, as
it is picturesquely called, has been feelingly written in recent
times by Fowler, Herbert, Partridge, Gowers, and others. It
is a fascinating and melancholy theme, but is outside the
scope and alien to the theme of this book.

Memorable writing – that is, literature – draws upon, or,
more precisely, reflects the past in another way. A representative anthology of English prose, the *Oxford Book*, for
example, is a kind of illustrative history of English syntax
and idiom. If we study a few individual passages reasonably
spaced in time we shall see how one convention, one mode
of expression, succeeds another. Literature, as distinct from
ephemeral writing and officialese, preserves what is best and
most worthy out of the past and hands it on as a living tradition; and since it has permanence, we are conscious of the
continuity. We are conscious too that the principles and
rules which govern 'modern usage' are often upset by the
example of literature; and for this very reason, that all literature written before our own age inevitably reflects a usage
that is not modern; the past impinges on the present. Every
writer upon what is called 'good English' has to recognize,
though he may be embarrassed by this simple fact; and also
to realize that, even in the realm of written (as distinct from
spoken) English, the present slips into the past. His book
grows out of date even as he writes it. The 'best English'
transcends the particular contemporary period; it both
determines and is determined by the usage and custom of
succeeding generations, and represents the composite usage
of them all.

2

It so happened that just as I sat down to draft this chapter
the BBC critics were settling down to discuss Mr Eric Partridge's *The Concise Usage and Abusage*. So I put aside pen
and paper and listened. Miss C. V. Wedgwood opened the

discussion. She observed that we talk nowadays of usage rather than rules, because rules are broken by so many good writers. Shakespeare, for example, was guilty of the double comparative; Defoe and Addison of the confused and mis-related participle. The truth was (she continued) that English grammar is accommodating, and has only one rule, that it should be clear. Ours is a democratic language, and affords us a freedom we ought not to abuse. Thus, with platitude and half-truth, she pronounced upon English and Mr Partridge. Others then began to join in. The chairman ventured the remark that 'nobody bothers to write grammatically', and declared that for her part she was not inclined to submit to correction. Another confessed that, having been accustomed to using tautology and literarisms, he was going to stick to them. A third asked who the book was for and was silently rebuked by a fourth, who managed to slip in the phrase 'for whom the book is written'. A fifth summed it all up in the ponderous statement that 'language must be the servant of the thought'. And so they passed on to Art.

They were, although they did not appear to notice it, touching upon this profound and difficult subject of the relationship of literature to language. I have shown in *The Pattern of English* that with the development, about the end of the seventeenth century, of what we more specifically call modern prose, there came a consciousness of right and wrong; in Dryden, for example, who condemned the preposition at the end of a sentence, and in Steele, whose *Petition of 'Who' and 'Which'* sought to determine the proper use of various forms of the relative pronoun. The grammarians of the next century or so – Lowth, Murray, Cobbett, in particular – tended, in their treatment of syntax, to the formulation of dogmatic rules. Their influence persisted until the beginning of the twentieth century. Nesfield, whose books belong to that period, may legitimately be called a grammarian of the rigid school; but it is significant that even he admitted certain compromises and modifications which, by recognizing practice as well as theory, pointed the way to the modern approach through usage. The emphasis moved from what, theoretically, ought to be, to what – however deplorable it might appear – in many writers undoubtedly was.

Grammatical dogmatism left us a legacy of superstitions, of which Dryden's condemnation of the preposition-at-end is an outstanding example. Ironically, in language (as indeed in other matters) rules have a fascination for most of us. We like to be able to distinguish black from white, and are suspicious of the neutral tones. But rule and custom are not separate or separable conceptions. The writer on usage, like the older type of grammarian, is a teacher rather than a mere recorder. On the face of it, he declares that this is right, or wrong, not according to some abstract law or principle but because custom has made it so. But usage has a way of rounding on him. If custom, or usage, does determine the shape of the sentence, the turn of a phrase, the defiance of formal grammar, the choice of a word, it should be frankly recognized as the arbiter. This is no more than to say 'Whatever is, is right'. And there the modern grammarian (to use a convenient but misleading term) quite naturally and on the whole justly demurs. He must harness usage to some kind of established rule or principle. This, he declares, is what thousands of people say or write, this crops up again and again in reputable newspapers and magazines – nevertheless it is wrong and therefore to be avoided. It is clear that in his mind sheer custom, the actual practice of those who use the language, has not the last word; it must be judged, and if necessary condemned, by some academic and nebulous tribunal of grammar. He is quite often proved wrong. Custom wins, and (if he lives long enough) he has to eat his words in a new edition. As a matter of fact, in English, which is not controlled by an Academy, it is usage that in the end prevails. A construction once very common may fall out of use; another long recognized may be frowned upon for some alleged ambiguity or awkwardness; another may come newly into favour. Over a long period the people who use the language fashion it, syntax, vocabulary, and idiom. The writer on usage, being (usually) intent upon guiding and teaching his contemporaries, isolates a particular period, his own. He is perfectly aware that the past confounds him, and that the future will outwit him. Meanwhile, he is content to make his record, and in so doing impose upon what might be a dangerous freedom a healthy discipline. Like other dealers in a living language, he cannot fully relate what is with what has gone before and what is likely to follow after. In a real sense he writes for today; but his book is also concerned with yesterday and tomorrow.

'Who is it for?' asked one of the critics referred to (in the first paragraph of section 2). The answer is, for the man or woman who wishes to converse well and with dignity, to write a letter, to draft a report, to write a leading article, a short story, a review, a critical essay; for all, in fact, who have occasion to write either voluntarily or perforce, to use English seriously for private or public communication. Fowler and Partridge and one or two others are not far from my elbow as I write this chapter. At any time, halting between two opinions, I may need their help and guidance. They are the guardian angels, as it were, of a language that, in the hands of most of us, is only too apt to fall into evil ways. Whenever the sentence becomes a little entangled, or a construction gets us in two minds, we hear the beating of their wings.

But behind that innocent question there was an honest doubt as well as (it must be confessed) a covert sneer. It is fairly plain that the critics themselves felt a little above *The Concise Usage and Abusage*. For whomever else it was, it was not for them. And we all, pondering the first clause of my last sentence, share their doubts. English, we murmur, is democratic, free, untrammelled by 'grammar'. There is a natural language, and a 'grammatical' language, and they do not always agree. 'Who is it for?' and 'Whoever else it is for?', being natural, are right. It is not a mere modern belief, a fashionable and facile acceptance of 'grammar without tears', but originates from an idea that when English lost its inflections it lost what we may call its central mechanism. In the *Grammar* which Johnson prefixed to his *Dictionary*

(1755) he devotes about fourteen lines to syntax, the art of constructing sentences and putting them together. 'Our language,' he says blandly, 'has so little inflection or variety of terminations, that its construction neither requires nor admits many rules.' Once the bugbear of agreement was out of the way, syntax or construction could be left to look after itself.

In all this there is both truth and fallacy. Johnson was not, in fact, so far off the mark as we, living in the post-Fowler age, imagine him to be. The language of his time had greater freedoms than ours, as I have shown in my treatment of the participle phrase in *The Pattern of English* (pp. 67 ff.). The grammarians were only just beginning to study the language as it was written, in the main by great writers, and to consider not so much its accidence as its syntax. As I have already pointed out, the process was slow and did not come to fruition till our own century, But now that it has come to fruition, and we have been made conscious of those 'rules' which Johnson said were not required, we cannot ignore them. It is because Johnson was not conscious of them that his statement contains an element of truth; its fallacy, or (more precisely) its inadequacy, is only observable in the light of the present.

But even for the ordinary writer today a question remains – whether this emphasis on what I have called the 'mechanism' of the language is either helpful or desirable. We may well ask whether it does not tend to set a gulf between speech and writing, to interfere with the natural and legitimate impact of the colloquial upon the written language, to set a brake, as it were, upon spontaneity. Whatever the answers to these questions may be – and they are given, often indirectly, at various places in this book – it is certain that the modern treatment of usage has set people thinking· about English for its own sake. To that the arguments in office or school and much correspondence in the Press are abundant testimony. On the whole, it is a good thing that, as we sit down to write, we are aware of at least some of the pitfalls, and may, with a little concentrated study and persistent reference, avoid most of them. True, like Andrew Lang, we are almost afraid to put pen to paper; but a healthy fear may be, after all, better than a slapdash or careless abandon.

And yet – we have not quite settled the question. All this time we have been moving in the realm of 'good' and 'better' English, that which can hope to escape serious criticism and send away baffled 'the reader over our shoulder'. Most of us are like Alice in confusing 'I say what I mean' with 'I mean what I say'. To the writer of workaday prose – to you and me – the ways of words themselves are difficult to follow, and the proper ordering of them a perplexing business. Our difficulty is to make them say what we mean: to bridge the gap between thought and the expression of it in speech or writing. This very metaphor, by the way, begs a question, as we shall see later; but for the moment it may stand. As Keats said in the very act of writing a poem, 'the dull brain perplexes and retards', by which he meant that the very mechanism of language got in the way of inspiration. That is, as we all know in our less exalted way, always true, since language is, at best, an imperfect instrument. Only we try to make it as perfect as possible by studying and, as far as we are able, putting into practice certain rules and principles that govern, or seem to govern, it.

But what of the creative writer, the man who achieves what we call literature? Keats himself suggests that he has difficulties; but is he aware of that mechanism of which we are all too painfully conscious? The answer is that though he recognizes the general pattern of English, with the details, the specific points of grammar and usage which fill the pages of Fowler and Partridge, he is not primarily, or consciously, concerned. True, this is to make a somewhat reckless generalization; but it is, on the whole, justified. And for this reason. The creative writer's thought – vital, urgent, imaginative – seeks an expression in language that is worthy of it, and most aptly represents it. His search is often arduous, for his thought does not, any more than ours, automatically jump the gap that separates it from expression, as we may see if we study the original manuscript of a literary work.

Yet, in another sense, thought and expression are one; this means that literature is written in a language whose very texture is determined by the thought and the feeling of the writer. In the process of this coalescence what we think of as 'correctness' sometimes goes by the board. The man (or woman) who is inspired to write a great book does not consciously write, as we say, by the book.

So we arrive at a paradox – that the 'best English' cannot be equated with 'good English' in the ordinary sense; it transcends it. Not that this must be exaggerated. In the nature of things, if he is to make his thought clear to the reader, the writer must follow, in the main, accepted usage. 'Nobody bothers to write grammatically', said the chairman of the Critics. It was a foolish as well as a fatuous remark. They do; they always did – if, that is, we admit the liberal and reasonable interpretation of 'grammatically'. But the writer of literature, the 'best English', is not a slave to grammar; in fact, he will usually confess, almost with pride, that he knows nothing about it. But, since he is a writer of literature, he has an instinct for language, which includes (although he is loth to admit it) its grammar. With this instinct, however, goes another – the instinct for the æsthetic quality of the sentence and the paragraph. And these two instincts do not always agree. There is not so much a war between them as a healthy tension: and it is, in fact, this very tension that is at the very heart of the 'best English'.

This brings us again to the element of time. Since our language is living, usage has continually changed over the period we shall consider, some 450 years, and is, indeed, still changing. The vocabulary, accidence, syntax, and idiom of Shakespeare's or Dr Johnson's time are not the same as ours. For this reason, we are not entitled to say that Shakespeare's or Dr Johnson's grammar is bad, or (with Cobbett) that 'Milton is a writer who has committed many hundreds, if not thousands, of grammatical errors'. We are measuring with our own measuring-rod something which it is not competent to measure. For that measuring-rod is our knowledge or conception of what Fowler rightly called 'modern usage'. We are considering English at a particular point of time, our own; and, even so, it is undergoing changes year by year, almost (especially in vocabulary and idiom) day by day. No writer of literature can properly be judged except by the standard of usage as it was in his own period – a usage which, as we learned from Doctor Johnson (p. 17), was not codified until modern times. Thus an author of the not very distant past may not only offend against some of the syntactical principles which we know from Fowler or Partridge, but he may commit what we should consider actual solecisms, as when Cowper writes 'Yourself was one of the last of my female relations that I saw before I went to St Albans', or Fielding 'a lady who had already rode more than forty miles'. They were living and writing at a time when 'yourself was' (for 'you were') and *rode* (for *ridden*) were customary expressions; and there is nothing more to be said.

A fairly large dictionary (like the *Shorter Oxford*), and indeed good concise dictionaries, recognize the changing usage in modern English. In the main they record, without any comment except that a particular construction, once common and accepted, is obsolescent, or a mild warning that it is not considered good English now. That is a thing to remember when we seek guidance from the writers on modern usage, who themselves often, by the way, invoke the past especially against grammatical superstitions. In brief, it is important to distinguish between modern English, by which we mean the language from the sixteenth century onwards, and current English, the language of today.[1]

So much for time. There are two other factors to be taken into account, both of which are specifically dealt with in later chapters (V–VII). The first is that a writer may express himself in one of two ways – prose or verse; and that since verse has special qualities of its own, like rhyme and metre, its syntax differs somewhat from that of prose. The second is

[1] Fowler's term 'modern English usage' (that is, the usage of current English) is nevertheless retained as not being open to serious misunderstanding.

that a writer may hammer out for himself a particular style of writing (as, for example, Carlyle did), and in doing so may defy the customary usage of his own age. As we shall see from time to time in this book, the writer's aim, the form he chooses, his subject – all these have to be taken into account. To some extent (but not entirely) he lives in a linguistic world of his own, whose laws and customs may not in every respect correspond with those of the more mundane world of grammar and the mechanics of language.

That very phrase, 'the mechanics of language', brings us down to earth again. In this difficult business of relating a changing language to its literature – and, indeed, in general – the terms 'grammar' and 'usage' are inadequate and may be misleading. They imply at once a contrast and an identity. Sometimes we are apt to think that usage defies, and sometimes that it fashions, grammar. The single term 'syntactical grammar' is better, signifying a manner or way of writing which is related more closely than 'idiom' in its wider sense ('form of expression peculiar to a language' – COD) to normal syntax. It has the advantage that it suggests a certain freedom of construction, and has no relation to the usage of a particular period. In applying it to creative writing we throw away, when necessary or expedient, our measuring-rod, and (to use a doubtful but useful metaphor of today) give the writer an alibi. We recognize, in fact, that he has a freedom which we indulge in only at our peril; he is like a Test cricketer who, having mastered all the laws, principles, and niceties of batsmanship, now and then in a moment of inspiration forgets them all in one glorious sweep to the boundary.

CHAPTER II

VOCABULARY

'PROSE,' SAID Coleridge, 'consists of the right words in the right order.' It seems a singularly naïve and inadequate definition from so metaphysical a thinker, but at least it reminds us that ultimately the words of the language are the tools, as it were, of the creative writer as they are of us all. He has to recognize their form, their grammatical function, and their meaning according to the usage of his own time. Since the middle of the eighteenth century their form – that is, their spelling – has been fixed; but up to that time it was, within certain limits, variable. This means that a piece of literature written, say, in the seventeenth century will contain spellings that, by our standards, are wrong. Here, by way of example, is a familiar passage from one of Bacon's Essays:

> If a Man Write little, he had need haue a Great memory; If he Conferre little, he had need haue a Present Wit; And if he Reade little, he had need haue much Cunning, to seeme to know that, he doth not. *Histories* make Men Wise; *Poets* Witty; The *Mathematicks* Subtill; *Naturall Philosophy* deepe; *Morall* Graue; *Logick* and *Rhetorick* Able to Content. *Abeunt studia in Mores.* Nay there is no Stond or Impediment in the Wit, but may be wrought out by *Fit Studies*: Like as Diseases of the Body, may haue Appropriate Exercises.

True, the spelling does not differ noticeably from our own; but it differs sufficiently to give the prose a novel appearance to the eye, an appearance whose novelty is emphasized by the use of initial capitals in many words, and by the punctuation. In our judgement of the best English of the distant past we cannot discount these outward qualities; they are part of its texture. Of punctuation and the use of capitals more is said in a later chapter (VI). The actual spelling that differs from our own has no great linguistic significance in itself; but it does suggest, what is probably true, that the pronunciation of the seventeenth century was more deliberate, less blurred and clipped, than it is today. Since, in prose as well as in poetry, the actual sound of the words is an important element, it is something which must be taken into consideration; and if spelling, however remotely, suggests a sound that does not altogether correspond with modern pronunciation, it cannot be discounted. To read a piece of prose, like the one just quoted, as it was originally written is to see it and hear it in a slightly different way. We may realize this more clearly if we take a still more familiar passage, this time from the Authorized Version of the Bible (1611):

Remember now thy Creatour in the dayes of thy youth, while the euil daies come not, nor the yeeres drawe nigh, when thou shalt say, I *haue* no pleasure in them: While the Sunne, or the light, or the moone, or the starres be not darkened, nor the cloudes returne after the raine: In the day when the keepers of the house shall tremble, and the strong men shall bowe themselues, and the grinders cease, because they are fewe, and those that looke out of the windowes be darkened: And the doores shal be shut in the streets, when the sound of the grinding is low, and he shall rise vp at the voice of the bird, and all the daughters of musicke shall be brought low.[1]

It is not too much to say that when we read those words so printed and punctuated they strike us afresh with a new sound, almost with a new meaning. Indeed, no doubt on the lips of the translators themselves and the people who first read them aloud in church they actually had a different sound from that which we associate with them. For the very reason that sound and even meaning have some relation to form it is a good thing to read, when possible, a book in the original text.[2] The 'best English' is apt to be spoilt by the attentions of the modernizer and the editor.

[1] *Ecclesiastes* xii.

[2] For the relationship of sound and rhythm, and the general treatment of sound in the sentence, see Chapter VI.

Of the writer's attitude to grammatical function of words enough has already been said in Chapter I and in *The Pattern of English*. His syntactical idiom in the use of an individual word – in deciding, for example, the construction that is appropriate to it – will to some extent depend (as does everything else) on the usage of his own time, and will be based on both colloquial and literary practice, with the emphasis now on the one and now on the other. In particular, he will be alert to that flexibility of function which is characteristic of English, by which a single word can in its time play many parts, often facilitating economy and conciseness of expression. In English which is truly living and vital the conventional divisions of the parts of speech are often ignored at the bidding of thought and in the interests of vividness or clarity.

When we come to meaning, we are in deeper water. We have only to consult a modern dictionary to realize that in the course of some 450 years most words, including even connectives like conjunctions and prepositions, have acquired various meanings and nuances of meaning in addition to what may be called their primary sense. The acquired meanings arise ultimately from the primary sense by a process of simple association often linked with metaphor. Thus the word *head* means primarily the top organ of the body, and from that develop all kinds of associated senses signifying 'topness' – the head of a bed, a river, a boil, a page, a staircase, an axe, a glass of liquor, or – with a further metaphorical development and the added association of the head with intellectual power – signifying a principal, as the head of a firm or of a school. Thus the word grows during the centuries; it is a living part of a living language. Like a tree it puts forth branches, its branches being idioms and sometimes new syntactical functions. We use, for example, the phrase 'come to a head' literally of a boil but figuratively or metaphorically of an abstract thing like trouble or a quarrel. Every sizeable dictionary contains, besides the actual definitions of words, idiomatic phrases in which they occur, where ordinary definition cannot follow them. In a living language words never become merely static, never continue in one stay. Their form, their function, and their sense (with all that is implied in that term) have their far-spreading roots in the past of our own and other languages. In considering them we have both to relate and to separate yesterday and today.

This 'livingness' of words is closely associated with, and partially explained by, the rich and complicated structure of the vocabulary of the language. Basically, English is English; that is, its original vocabulary consists of those words which were native to the peoples – Angles, Jutes, and Saxons – who occupied this island during the sixth century, with a number of borrowings from Latin, a few from the Celts or British, whom the 'English' invaders displaced, and a few from the Danes, who tried to displace them. But in the centuries following the Norman Conquest there came a great influx of French words as the conquerors settled down with the conquered. Later, reflecting the growing complexities of life and thought, came a multitude of words from Latin and Greek. And during its history English has assimilated or borrowed[1] words from most of the other languages of the world. It is, perhaps, significant that the English language is the one truly international institution at present existing.

Now, out of this jostling of words through the centuries come one or two interesting results. The first is that many words, most of them old native ones, get pushed out altogether. But not only these. There is, in fact, a continual wastage, so that a word which was current in literature in, say, the eighteenth or even the nineteenth century, may now be obsolete. Fashion, indeed, comes into the matter, as it does with clothes; a word, like a garment, may go quite out of fashion, and so disappear. The words that get completely lost, however, are comparatively few, even if we go back to King Alfred's time. More important and far-reaching is the

---

[1] By assimilation is meant fashioning the word to an English form and giving it an English sense; by borrowing, taking the word as it stands (like *fauteuil* from French or *allegro* from Italian), though not always with the sense it had in the original language.

second result, which affects the whole structure and texture of the language, and its literature.

Briefly it is this. Since our vocabulary, gathered from so many sources, is unusually rich, and continually grows as the language grows, it follows that the sense of most words which have had a long life and are still living is affected, at various stages of the language, by later derivatives with approximately the same sense. In the jostling they are not knocked out of existence, but knocked about, reshaped, as it were, by their new neighbours. A condition of survival is that words closely related in sense adjust themselves to one another, so that no two of them have precisely the same nuance or range of meaning. This adjustment is obviously a gradual and continuing process; it will not have advanced so far in, say, the eighteenth as in the twentieth century. It follows that the literature of some four hundred and fifty years will reflect the sometimes obvious, but more often subtle changes of meaning that words have undergone.

This is only one way of stating a fairly obvious fact, that language continually accommodates itself to life. A word comes into the vocabulary when it is needed to represent a certain object or to express a certain concept. Until that object appears, or that concept forms itself in the minds of men, the word for it does not exist, and obviously cannot be found in the literature that ante-dates its existence. In his philosophical novel *Rasselas* Doctor Johnson speaks of a man who had discovered the art of flying. Rasselas, coming one day to amuse himself in his usual manner, found the man 'busy in building a sailing chariot' to which afterwards he added 'many ingenious contrivances to facilitate motion, and unite levity with strength', and to which he finally gave wings. But Johnson had no single word to represent this novel machine. That was to come later, in a number of different forms – *airship*, *aeroplane*, *aircraft*. If, indeed, Johnson himself had invented a word, as he might have done, it is conceivable that it might have entered the language then, and finally established itself, as some words have done that were coined by imaginative or creative writers.

But as it was, though he was peeping into the future, he contented himself with the vocabulary of his own period. In the same way H. G. Wells, writing in the year 1903, anticipated the military contrivance which about thirteen years later actually made its appearance on the battlefield and was christened a 'tank'. But he did not, and could not be expected to, invent the word, which arose (like many others) in the speech of ordinary men. His name for the machine was 'land iron-clad'.

The vocabulary of a language is, therefore, in a sense dated, especially those words in it which represent material things. Of course, the modern writer, standing at this point of history, can use all the words that have accumulated up to the present. But as we go back in time the available vocabulary is necessarily smaller because the life which it reflected, with all its manifold activities, was not so highly or widely developed. No writer before this century could have used hundreds of words that are familiar to us today. There are, in particular, watersheds in language as there are in history. The Industrial Revolution was one of them. It quite sharply divides the vocabulary of the literature before it from that which came after it. Our own age is another. The unexampled developments in thought, social conditions, political outlook, and scientific invention, that have taken place since the outbreak of the Second World War (1939) have separated, at any rate to some extent, the vocabulary – and therefore the literature – of today from that even of the immediate yesterday. That is true not only of new words, but of old words with a new meaning. The modern reader or writer cannot but attach to such words as *jet*, *atom*, *welfare*, *alert*, *appeasement*, *cold*, *hot* a sense that did not belong to them some twenty years ago. When we read the literature of the past, we think of some, at least, of its words in not quite the same way as the writer thought of them; in the process of time they have taken on new 'overtones', new shades of meaning. In vocabulary, as in syntax, literature and language are inextricably bound together.

To return, then, to Coleridge's definition. 'Proper words,'

he said, 'in the proper order.' The question at once arises,
'What is meant by "proper words"?' It is sometimes said
that since no two established words are identical in meaning
and use – that is, since there are no absolute synonyms – one
word, and one word only, will be appropriate to any given
context. As a rough principle enjoining on the ordinary
writer the necessity for a careful choice of words, this statement contains a modicum of truth. But only a modicum.
The words in any group of synonyms[1] so far correspond in
meaning as to be capable of use indiscriminately in some
contexts; yet at the same time each will have a nuance of
meaning, or a peculiarity of syntactical construction, that
for a particular context renders it suitable above all the
others. Moreover (though we are on dangerous ground
here), we may substitute for a single word a periphrasis – a
phrase, or even a clause. Words are not like counters, complete in themselves and independent of one another, or like
the pieces of a jigsaw puzzle. They are (it cannot be too often
emphasized) living things. Even in ordinary writing the Dictionary and the Thesaurus can help us only up to a certain
point. There is something beyond definition; and for the
creative writer a realm in which he walks by the light of his
intuition and imagination.

This does not imply that meaning is not itself of the first
importance. It must be so if, as we have postulated, the
writer's thought is crystallized in his expression. 'In all
speech,' says Ben Jonson, 'words and sense are as the body
and soul.' But there are other factors to be taken into
account. Time, as we have already seen, is one of them. A
writer is limited to the vocabulary as it is in his own period,
except in so far as he himself adopts and adapts new derivatives or actually invents new words. Another is sound, the
sound, that is, of an individual word in relation to its context.
This, in its turn, is bound up with the sound of the sentence –

---

[1] The word is used loosely here for closely related words, often of
different origins, which, isolated from any context, are not easily distinguishable for meaning. The reader is referred to Mr V. H. Collins's
two excellent books, *The Choice of Words* and *One Word and Another*.

its 'flow' or rhythm. To maintain this rhythm a writer may, for example, prefer at a given point in the sentence a three-syllabled to a two-syllabled word. There is an interesting example in the passage already quoted (p. 12) from Landor, where for the sake of cadence, the rise and fall of the sentence, he uses the word *appertain* instead of the simpler and more obvious *belong*. But this is a big subject, which is treated in detail in a later chapter (VI).

More generally, the choice of word depends upon the writer's theme and the type of literature he is creating – essay, biography, novel, and the rest; for this determines what may be called the texture of his prose. And here we have to recognize the all-important fact that every writer of literature, informed (as we imagine) by a creative spirit, fashions for himself a certain manner of writing, which is usually called style. This style is an individual thing, arising out of his own personality and dependent upon his peculiar genius; and it is, or should be, closely related to the matter he has in hand. The general subject of style is dealt with later on (Chapter VII); but as far as it affects the choice of word it may be treated here.

Once we are conscious of this element of style which is at the very heart of literature, whether prose or verse, we may interpret Coleridge's simple term 'proper' as signifying 'proper to the style'. In general, words are apt or evocative; that is, they may give us the mere sense of 'properness' or 'rightness' in their context, or they may in themselves, by their sound and a suggestiveness that derives from their complexities of meaning, evoke in us a certain æsthetic delight or emotion. It is a difference of degree, and it determines the effectiveness of individual words in the prose of which they are a part. Doctor Johnson said that a man who desired to write good prose would 'give his nights and days to Addison'. He was postulating a kind of norm, which does not, in fact, exist. But there is a prose style which, though it cannot be independent of the personality of its author, is free from idiosyncrasies and conforms to a general though indefinable type. It is in such prose that individual words

are apt rather than evocative. We are not conscious of them
except as they perfectly fit the context and are woven into the
texture of the sentence.

Any passage of Addison himself will illustrate this:

> It is certain the light talkative humour of the French has
> not a little infected their tongue, which might be shown
> by many instances; as the genius of the Italians, which
> is so much addicted to music and ceremony, has moulded
> all their words and phrases to their particular uses. The
> stateliness and gravity of the Spaniards shows itself to
> perfection in the solemnity of their language; and the
> blunt honest humour of the German sounds better in the
> roughness of the High-Dutch than it would in a politer
> tongue.

Now it is evident that here Addison has chosen his words
carefully: *talkative*, *genius*, *ceremony*, *stateliness*, *gravity*,
solemnity, *blunt*, they all express his meaning exactly and
contribute individually as well as by their relationships (of
balance or antithesis, for example) to the general effect of the
passage. But they do not of themselves evoke any particular
feeling in us. They are parts, though important and highly
significant parts, of a satisfyingly æsthetic whole.

It is, in general, true that as we travel farther from this
hypothetical norm, what is sometimes called 'the middle
style' – as we move, for example, from Addison to Lamb, or
from Trollope to Dickens – words tend to take on a more
evocative quality. To begin with, the vocabulary, taken as a
whole, may be the outstanding and most easily recognizable
element in a particular style. Thus we can make a rough and
somewhat reckless division between those writers who confine themselves to a comparatively small stock of words,
many of them of native origin, and those who explore the
whole range of the available vocabulary, often with a prefer-
ence for the long and high-sounding word derived from the
Classical languages. And here we must pause to comment
upon what is called 'the Saxon heresy', because simplicity
or shortness is loosely equated with Saxon origin. It is often

said by writers on language (including Fowler himself) that of two possible words the shorter is always to be preferred. That may be a useful rough and ready rule for the ordinary writer who finds himself a little at sea outside certain limits of vocabulary, though it is based on a fallacy that takes no account of context.[1] In literature it does not apply at all, for reasons that have already been stated. The 'proper' word is no more the short than the long word; it is that which fits the style, and either by its aptness or its evocativeness, contributes to or heightens the general effect of a piece of prose.

It is, in fact, commonly stated that in any normal piece of literary prose the native words far outnumber the borrowings from Classical and other languages, provided every word is counted. Dr Sheard in *The Words We Use* quotes Emerson's calculation that 'Shakespeare has only ten per cent of borrowed words, Milton nineteen per cent, Johnson twenty-eight per cent, Gibbon thirty per cent, Tennyson twelve per cent, and the Bible (basing the count on three Gospels only) has no more than six per cent'. But of course the counting of every word materially affects these proportions, since nearly all the connectives (prepositions and conjunctions) and the pronouns are native. Nor does this in any way make the native word sacrosanct when the use of a borrowed word would make for conciseness or contribute to the rhythm and sound of the sentence.

It is true, however, that as far as vocabulary is concerned some prose leans to the simple, even the Saxon, and some to what for want of a better term may be called ornate. Both, the simple and the ornate, may have the quality of evocativeness because they are attuned to what the writer has to say, and are themselves an essential element in his manner of saying it. Of the simple style the Authorized Version of the Bible is often quoted as an example; but this is rather less than a half-truth. There are, as Mr Somerset Maugham has reminded us, other qualities in it, 'those rhythms, that powerful vocabulary, that grandiloquence', which set it in a

[1] Of this Fowler's article on *Genteelism* (MEU) is a curious and disturbing example.

category of its own. Let us turn instead to what Robert Southey called 'the home-spun' of Bunyan, though it must be admitted that the greatest influence on the moulder of Bunyan's style was this same Authorized Version. Still, Bunyan was, in birth and upbringing, not indeed an uneducated but basically a simple man; and in his writing, though it is often eloquent and sometimes falls into 'those rhythms', sometimes even hovers on the brink of grandiloquence, he uses a vocabulary that is powerful because it is, in the main, drawn from established native or long-assimilated words:

> Now they had not gone far, but a great mist and darkness fell upon them all, so that they could scarce, for a great while, see the one the other; wherefore they were forced, for some time, to feel for one another by words, for they walked not by sight.
>
> The way also was here very wearisome, through dirt and slabbiness. Nor was there on all this ground so much as one inn or victualling house, therein to refresh the feebler sort. Here, therefore, there was grunting, and puffing, and sighing. While one tumbleth over a bush, another sticks fast in the dirt; and the children, some of them, lost their shoes in the mire.

Now it is obvious that here the very homeliness of the words – *darkness*, *dirt*, *slabbiness*, *grunting*, *puffing*, *sighing* – plays a great part in creating the atmosphere of the narrative. To put it another way, the words are evocative as well as apt to their context. They suggest that undefinable something which is a little beyond meaning.

By way of contrast, let us go to a writer somewhat before Bunyan, who out of a scholarly and fantastic mind evolved quite a different kind of prose:

> There is nothing strictly immortal, but immortality. Whatever hath no beginning, may be confident of no end; – all others have a dependent being and within the reach of destruction; – which is the peculiar of that necessary

essence that cannot destroy itself; – and the highest strain of omnipotency, to be so powerfully constituted as not to suffer even from the power of itself. But the sufficiency of Christian immortality frustrates all earthly glory, and the quality of either state after death, makes a folly of posthumous memory. God who can only destroy our souls, and hath assured our resurrections, either of our bodies or names hath directly promised no duration. Wherein there is so much of chance, that the boldest expectants have found unhappy frustration; and to hold long subsistence, seems but a scape in oblivion.

Again it is the words themselves, classical polysyllables – *immortality, dependent, omnipotency, posthumous, resurrection, expectants, frustration, oblivion* – that have a strange impact upon our imagination. In fact, as we read certain passages in *Hydriotaphia* we are so mesmerized by them that we tend to lose, or forget, the meaning – if, indeed, there is any. We are reminded that words, properly used, are never mere counters. They communicate not only with our minds, but also with our hearts and emotions.

But we cannot properly speak in terms of black and white, drawing a fixed line between the simple and the ornate vocabulary. Authors lean, in general, to one or the other, or take the middle way; but they all draw upon a store of words that is adequate to their subject, trespassing from time to time upon one another's domain. Bunyan, for example, is on occasions by no means averse to the polysyllable – as witness some of his names like 'the *Celestial* City' and 'the *Delectable* Mountains'; and Sir Thomas Browne's vocabulary can be simple: 'Our fathers find their graves in our short memories, and sadly tell us how we may be buried in our survivors. Grave-stones scarce tell truth forty years. Generations pass while some trees stand, and old families last not three oaks.' In the course of a book, or even so short a thing as an essay, manner changes with mood or theme; and the vocabulary reflects the nature of that change.

It is clear, then, that in all literature, the choice of words, the range of the vocabulary commonly favoured by the writer, has a general effect of aptness or evocativeness. From it any piece of prose acquires a particular flavour. But we may also consider the effect of words individually; and here we have to remember that only certain types, or (to speak in grammatical terms) certain parts of speech, are more potent and significant than others. In the first chapter of *A Writer's Notes on His Trade* C. E. Montague bewails the undeniable fact that in any coherent sentence there must be particles, as distinct from words, which are not vines, but only 'props in the vineyard'. Why, he says, should not the symbols that a writer has to use 'be cut free from their baggage of lengthiness and their cumbrous rules of construction? Why should a glowing sentence have to be dulled with such lack-lustre dust as all the "its" and "is" and "that" and "which" and "to" that clog it? When all is done that a man can do, what a quantity of dull setting there has had to be for each gem that he has cut! At best, how much of matter to how little of form!' Montague, writing in the 1920's, could not foresee that later writers, in both verse and prose, impatient of 'such lack-lustre dust', would indeed do their best to get rid of it, even in defiance of normal syntax. However, the fact remains that in the structure of the 'coherent sentence' such particles are necessary, and, strip the sentence as bare as you will, they cannot entirely be dispensed with. Moreover, the vine needs props, and the props themselves must be in their rightful place; or, to drop the metaphor, the particles must contribute not only to the structure but also to the rhythm of the sentence.

The significant or evocative words are nouns, main (as distinct from auxiliary) verbs, adjectives and adverbs. It is by his choice and use of these that the writer achieves the 'glowing sentence', as Montague has it; achieves also the effective sentence, where the words are not so much evocative as apt. Indeed it is in the plainer, more normal, prose, unheightened by any deliberate effects of colour, that the choice of words, though less obvious, is more subtle – in a passage of Hazlitt, for example, or Jane Austen, or Matthew Arnold. The 'glowing sentence' (it is a somewhat unfortunate term) is best illustrated from descriptive prose. Here, by way of example, are two passages, the first from Thomas Hardy's *Far From the Madding Crowd*, the other from John Ruskin's *The Stones of Venice*:

The sky was clear – remarkably clear – and the twinkling of all the stars seemed to be but throbs of one body, timed by a common pulse. The North star was directly in the wind's eye, and since evening the Bear had swung round it outwardly to the east, till he was now at a right angle with the meridian. A difference of colour in the stars – oftener read of than seen in England – was really perceptible here. The kingly brilliancy of Sirius pierced the eye with a steely glitter, the star called Capella was yellow, Aldebaran and Betelgueux shone with a fiery red.

To persons standing alone on a hill during a clear midnight such as this, the roll of the world eastward is almost a palpable movement. The sensation may be caused by the panoramic glide of the stars past earthly objects, which is perceptible in a few minutes of stillness, or by the better outlook upon space that a hill affords, or by the wind, or by the solitude; but whatever be its origin, the impression of riding along is vivid and abiding.

Let us go together up the more retired street, at the end of which we can see the pinnacles of one of the towers, and then through the low grey gateway, with its battlemented top and small latticed window in the centre, into the inner private-looking road or close, where nothing goes in but the carts of the tradesmen who supply the bishop and the chapter, and where there are little shaven grass-plots, fenced in by neat rails, before old-fashioned groups of somewhat diminutive and excessively trim houses, with little oriel and bay windows jutting out here and there, and deep wooden cornices and eaves painted cream colour and white, and small porches to their doors in the shape of cockle-shells, or little, crooked, thick, indescribable wooden gables warped a little on one side;

and so forward till we come to larger houses, also old-fashioned, but of red brick, and with gardens behind them, and fruit walls, which show here and there, among the nectarines, the vestiges of an old cloister arch or shaft, and looking in front on the cathedral square itself, laid out in rigid divisions of smooth grass and gravel walk, yet not uncheerful, especially on the sunny side, where the canons' children are walking with their nurserymaids.

In the Hardy passage the evocativeness of individual words is at once apparent – nouns like *brilliancy*, *glide*, *stillness*, *solitude*; proper names, *Sirius*, *Capella*, *Aldebaran*, *Betelgueux*, used almost as a poet like Milton would use them; adjectives like *sovereign*, *steely*, *panoramic*, *palpable*; verbs like *swung*, and *pierced*. Ruskin's nouns and verbs are less striking, though still effective. He relies rather on the adjective, or more especially a collocation of adjectives – 'little, crooked, thick, indescribable wooden gables'. There is indeed this difference in vocabulary between the two passages: Hardy is precise, while Ruskin tends to be lavish. It is a difference of economy.

This matter of economy or precision is all-important. There is such a thing as word intoxication. In the sixteenth century writers were attracted by what were called 'inkhorn terms', the new words, and even invented derivatives of them, that were pouring in from the Classical languages at that time. Shakespeare (himself by no means immune) has a gibe at them in *Love's Labour's Lost*. Many writers since then have been fascinated by words in themselves, whether inkhorn terms, or picturesque nouns and adjectives, or plain Saxon monosyllables. The trouble is that once the writer is even mildly word-intoxicated the words themselves begin to take charge. There is a gap between the thought and the expression; the pen of the ready writer, dripping with significant nouns and adjectives, runs away from (and with) the meaning. And this impairs what is, after all, at the heart of literature – sincerity. The writer, mesmerized by his own symbols, no longer says quite what he means. We have already hinted (p. 33) that this is true, on occasions, of even so great a prose-writer as Sir Thomas Browne. It may also be true of writers who are not so much intoxicated by words as over-fastidious in their use of them – like Walter Pater or Robert Louis Stevenson. Words are, at best, an inadequate means of communication; when they get out of hand they may even separate the writer from the reader.

Yet there is another side; and again Mr Somerset Maugham and C. E. Montague have something to say. Mr Maugham observes that Fowler 'did not see that simplicity may sometimes make concessions to euphony'; and goes on, 'I do not think a far-fetched, an archaic or even an affected word is out of place when it sounds better than the blunt, obvious one or when it gives the sentence a better balance'. He implies that the writer may be a little off the mark, a trifle imprecise, in the interests of rhythm; though he does hasten to add that nothing must obscure the meaning – 'anything is better than not to write clearly'. Here C. E. Montague is somewhat at odds with him. He has a whole chapter called 'Only too clear', the main argument of which is that in imaginative literature, because it is imaginative, individual words or expressions of which they form a part may have a meaning that the reader has to search for. The writer 'will, in a moderate sense of the term, have his non-lucid intervals. At times he will make us wrestle a little with him, in the dark, before he yields his full meaning, as God made the patriarch wrestle with the angel, to the patriarch's ultimate advantage', This is another way of saying that words may be evocative, not only in giving æsthetic delight to the reader by their sound, their power of suggestion, and even their very form, but also by 'teasing him into thought'.

The element of sound for sound's sake, or onomatopoeic effect, is far less common in prose than it is in poetry. Yet, as we have already seen, the quality of evocativeness does in some measure depend upon it. When we read the simple and moving sentence of Bunyan, 'So he passed over, and all the trumpets sounded for him on the other side', we are conscious that it is the very sound of the word *trumpets* that lends to it something of its magic. Certain words, indeed, have a natural, as distinct from an artificial onomatopoeic effect in their appropriate context; they strike on the ear and set up a kind of answering chord in the imagination. *Sound* itself is one of them, as, for example, in the sentence 'And his voice was as the sound of many waters'. So is the word *sea*, with its natural sibilant; and so (to steal some examples from Montague) are *burnish, crozier, lustre, beatitude, dawn*, together with many polysyllabic words like *intolerable* and *voluminous* whose syllables pile up, as it were, on the ear. Yet the sound cannot be divorced from meaning; or, to put it another way, the word is phonologically effective only as it fits the context. For example, the word *sound* has no evocativeness of sound when it is used in its other sense – 'a sound argument', 'a sound proposition'. There is a story told of J. A. Spender, the Editor of the *Westminster Gazette*, that when he was told that, in a literary competition, a majority of readers voted for *swallow* as the most evocatively sounding word in the language, he gurgled in his throat and enquired whether they meant that *swallow*. It is true, as Montague says, that in the sentence 'Then shall the dust return to the earth as it was', the very sound, even the form, of the word *dust* is evocative. But that is because it sets up certain trains of thought which are in themselves moving. When we say 'There was dust all over the table' the word has lost its strange evocative power.

In the best prose the sound effect of the individual word is never artificially contrived. It is there in the natural order of things; the word is the one the writer is inspired to choose, the 'proper' word in every sense, one that befits what we have called his sincerity. Tricks like alliteration, or sustained onomatopoeia, or echoic repetition are alien to prose. True, some writers do indulge in them; but their prose then takes on a new quality that gives it some affinity to verse. Here, however, we are on the verge of that no-man's-land that lies between prose and poetry, a territory to be explored in a later chapter (VI).

On the choice of words depends, too, the avoidance of

ugly sound, cacophony. Not that cacophony is a mortal sin. It may be a deliberate effect, closely allied to alliteration and onomatopoeia, and like them not appropriate to the nature and spirit of prose. But when it is not deliberate, it is unfortunate, a fault in the writer's general and it may be otherwise beautiful texture. It commonly arises when words of the same sound pattern – words, for example, ending in *-ation* or *-ness* or *-ly* – jostle together, so that, however clear or even pungent the meaning is, the ear is offended by an inadvertent rhyme or assonance. More especially it is the result of the clash of particles. Thus, it so happens that a number of these short but necessary words begin with *th* – the definite article, the plural pronoun *they*, the demonstrative pronouns and adjectives, including *that* with its various functions. The ordinary writer, if he has any ear, knows how easily this sound, recurring on words he cannot easily dispense with, has an effect not so much of cacophony as of dull monotony. In that very sentence, by the way, there is an example of the awkward assonance (*cacophony – monotony*); and a page or two back (p. 38) in the sentence beginning 'There is a story' two *thats* conspire to break whatever euphony it may have. Nor can the writer of the best English always escape the peril. The ubiquitous *th* is not easy to avoid, and a cluttering collocation of *ins* and *withs* and *tos* may play havoc with his finest periods. Yet in so far as he does not escape, his prose suffers. 'Many writers', says Mr Maugham, 'without distress will put two rhyming words together, join a monstrous long adjective to a monstrous long noun, or between the end of one word and the beginning of another have a conjunction of consonants that almost breaks your jaw.' He means without distress to himself, not to the reader; and implies that when his ear fails, his prose becomes less than memorable, falls even a little below literature.

There, then, are a few general principles. They cannot be adequately illustrated except from the vast body of prose literature itself. 'What do you read, my lord?' asked Polonius. 'Words, words, words,' said Hamlet. But Polonius was not satisfied – 'What is the matter, my lord?' Words and matter – they are not to be separated. In ordinary English, if it is at all adequate to its purpose, that correspondence holds; in the best English – literature – the matter is quickened into life by the words. Hamlet himself improvised a sentence or two of prose, almost as if to prove it: 'The satirical rogue says here that old men have grey beards, that their faces are wrinkled, their eyes purging thick amber and plum-tree gum, and that they have a plentiful lack of wit, together with most weak hams.' We are back with Coleridge again. There is, perhaps, in his definition more than meets the eye. It is recorded of a novelist that when he offered his publisher a novel of several thousand words the publisher replied laconically, 'What words, and in what order?' The story is, perhaps, apocryphal; but it would be pleasant to think it true. At any rate, it will serve as a moral with which to end this chapter.

CHAPTER III

FIGURE AND IMAGERY

MUCH HAS been written on the imagery of the poets, because imagery is an integral part of poetry, with a special significance of its own. When we read a book like Caroline Spurgeon's *Shakespeare's Imagery* we realize how closely the figure of speech, especially metaphor, is woven into the texture of the writing, as for example the recurrence of images of death and decay in *Hamlet*. For in poetry the effects are always heightened; the poet, 'giving to airy nothings a local habitation and a name' tends to see and think in pictures. The Road to Xanadu always leads, by devious and various ways, to the honey-dew and the milk of Paradise. One of the main differences between prose and poetry lies precisely here – that in prose imagery holds a subordinate place. To take a simple and somewhat superficial example: the long sustained simile, developed and elaborated for its own sake, a heritage of the Classical epic and hence sometimes called the 'Homeric simile', occurs at times in English poetry. We accept it as a deliberate and effective device. *Paradise Lost*, our one true English epic, abounds in such similes. But they are not confined to Milton. There is a famous example at the end of Matthew Arnold's *The Scholar Gipsy*:

> *Then fly our greetings, fly our speech and smiles!*
> *– As some grave Tyrian trader, from the sea,*
> *Descried at sunrise an emerging prow*
> *Lifting the cool-hair'd creepers stealthily,*
> *The fringes of a southward-facing brow*
> *Among the Aegean isles;*
> *And saw the merry Grecian coaster come,*
> *Freighted with amber grapes, and Chian wine,*
> *Green bursting figs, and tunnies steep'd in brine;*
> *And knew the intruders on his ancient home*

The young light-hearted Masters of the waves;
    And snatch'd his rudder, and shook out more sail,
        And day and night held on indignantly
O'er the blue Midland waters with the gale,
    Betwixt the Syrtes and soft Sicily,
        To where the Atlantic raves
Outside the Western Straits, and unbent sails
    There, where down cloudy cliffs, through sheets of foam,
    Shy traffickers, the dark Iberians come;
        And on the beach undid his corded bales.

Coming upon that, after reading the grave meditative stanzas of the poem, we are conscious of a kind of irrelevant revelance, of a short poem in its own right only half dependent on the rest, whose spirit is in the imagery itself. It is a device that only poetry can sustain.

For, in the main, such luxuries are alien to prose, which is in the full and literal sense of the term 'prosaic'. True, they sometimes occur – in Milton's own prose, for example; but when they do occur we have a feeling that prose is trespassing upon the domain of poetry. They are common, too, in the Authorized Version; but here again we know that the prose form into which the Hebrew (or the Greek) is translated has captured the poetry of the original:

> As an eagle stirreth up her nest, fluttereth over her young, spreadeth abroad her wings, taketh them, beareth them on her wings: so the Lord alone did lead him, and there was no strange god with him.

The simile, though not so elaborate as the true Homeric type, is developed, built up into a complete and sustained image. It is poetic, not prosaic; indeed, it occurs in a chapter which is headed 'The *Song* of Moses'. But how far the sustained, Homeric, simile stands outside the realm of prose as prose may be curiously illustrated from the work of one of our most famous novelists. Fielding, especially in *Tom Jones*, uses it as a comic device:

As when two doves, or two wood-pigeons, or as when Strephon and Phyllis (for that comes nearest to the mark) are retired into some pleasant solitary grove, to enjoy the delightful conversation of Love, that bashful boy, who cannot speak in public, and is never a good companion to more than two at a time; here, while every object is serene, should hoarse thunder burst suddenly through the shattered clouds, and rumbling roll along the sky, the frightened maid starts from the mossy bank or verdant turf, the pale livery of death succeeds the red regimentals in which Love had before drest her cheeks, fear shakes her whole frame, and her lover scarce supports her trembling tottering limbs.

Or as when two gentlemen, strangers to the wondrous wit of the place, are cracking a bottle together at some inn or tavern at Salisbury, if the great Dowdy, who acts the part of a madman as well as some of his setters-on do that of a fool, should rattle his chains, and dreadfully hum forth the grumbling catch along the gallery; the frightened strangers stand aghast; scared at the horrid sound, they seek some place of shelter from the approaching danger; and if the well-barred windows did admit their exit, would venture their necks to escape the threatening fury now coming upon them.

So trembled poor Sophia, so turned she pale at the noise of her father, who, in a voice most dreadful to hear, came on swearing, cursing, and vowing the destruction of Jones.

A special technique of poetry is there deliberately grafted on to a statement that is essentially, in the literary sense, prosaic, not for any heightened poetic or pseudo-poetic effect, but for one of quite a different kind – the effect of incongruity, which arises from the imposition of one medium on another.

The simple simile, however, belongs as much to prose as to poetry, to ordinary speech, in fact, as to any kind of writing. Whether spoken or written, it is a brief picture sometimes designed merely to explain, sometimes to illustrate, through the appeal of the familiar to the unfamiliar, the known to the unknown. When, for example, the Psalmist says, 'He giveth the snow like wool; he scattereth the hoar-frost like ashes', he is speaking as a shepherd[1] to shepherds, relating natural phenomena to objects that are closely bound up with their common life, the white shorn wool of the sheep, the white ashes of the camp-fire strewn on the grass. Some similes of this elemental type (rather comparisons, perhaps, than similes proper) have by long use in speech and writing become the small change of language – 'as white as snow', 'as brown as a berry', 'straight as a die', 'swift as an arrow', and the like. They are, indeed, mere clichés with very little life left in them. The difference between the simile in literature and the simile as we commonly use it in conversation and writing (as, for example, in a letter) is only one of degree; for the simile is the most natural of figures. It so happened that I broke off in the middle of this paragraph to go for a walk; and I met a neighbour of mine, an old man, who had had little or no education. In the course of our conversation he startled me with the following sentence: 'My father was always on the rocks and in abject poverty, but I, like a soldier waiting upon his commission or a priest upon his orders, always hoped for better things.' In his humility he addressed me, to my embarrassment, as 'an expert in English'. I told him that only in a very limited sense was that true; and that, in any case, he was something far better, one who could make his English living upon his tongue. He laughed as he went off to catch his bus; and I thought of him with a certain envy as I took up my pen again. I had already roughed out my next sentence in my mind before I met him; but it shall not see the light here. This shall take its place: it is with such aptness and vividness, yet at the same time naturalness, of simile that the writer makes his English living and effective upon the paper.

The normal signallers of the simile are the particles *like* and *as*. Very often, however, what appears to be a simile, thus

[1] Not necessarily David, of course. The term is used generally for a writer who may be assumed to be a countryman.

introduced, is no more than a comparison; there is no real image or picture, since like is likened to like. Thus when Defoe writes 'I feel like one pursued', he is merely making a kind of equation, in which one person imagines himself in the hypothetical condition of another. Certainly, to such an equation a picture may be added:

> once more
> I viewed the ocean green,
> And looked far forth, yet little saw
> Of what had else been seen,
>
> Like one that on a lonesome road
> Doth walk in fear and dread,
> And having once turned round, walks on,
> And turns no more his head;
> Because he knows a frightful fiend
> Doth close beside him tread.

But the picture here is strictly irrelevant to the comparison; it is a poetic ornament. The mariner is merely saying that he 'felt like one pursued'. We have a somewhat more elaborate example in the following passage from Milton, where two kinds of literary work are contrasted:

'. . . a work not to be rays'd from the heat of youth, or the vapours of wine, like that which flows at wast from the pen of some vulgar Amorist, or the trencher fury of a riming parasite.'

This type of comparison, verging on simile, is often used to express or illustrate actual size or dimension. Thus, when Swift describes Lilliputian objects he uses as a measuring-rod the ordinary objects of mankind: 'In the left there was a sort of engine, from the back of which were extended twenty long poles, resembling the palisades before your Majesty's court.' It is an explanatory figure rather than a piece of imagery.

Even at its simplest, the true simile is, like some words, evocative. It kindles the imagination:

Men fear *Death* as children fear to go in the dark.

At first sight, it seems that we have only a comparison of two kinds of fear; but, in fact, we have far more – the likeness of the man facing the dark unknown of death to the child frightened and bewildered in the actual darkness. The simple phrase, 'go in the dark', relates Man and the child in a single highly suggestive picture. A few other representative examples are given, each with its own brief comment:

1. She stood not dressed, but draped in pale antique folds, long and irregular like sculpture. – Charlotte Brontë.

What the three epithets *antique, long, irregular*, cannot quite achieve the simile is called in to do – to round off, as it were, the description. It is, in the first place, explanatory, the kind of simile we resort to in ordinary conversation. But it is more than that; it also suggests vividly the statuesque pose of the woman depicted. The sentence could end without it at *irregular*, but it would lose much of its effect; for the influence of the simile, though it comes so late, pervades the whole.

2. From the point of yonder rolling cloud I plunge into my past being, and revel there, as the sun-burnt Indian plunges headlong into the wave that wafts him to his native shore. – Hazlitt.

This simile is, in a general way, effective; but it does not quite bear analysis. Why the 'sun-burnt Indian', except, perhaps, for picturesqueness? Nor is the parallel between the writer's past being and the Indian's native shore quite valid. The simile rather blurs than lights up the statement, though until we consider it in detail, we are not conscious of this. Here is a more direct example from Hazlitt, where the images are topical and literary:

3. His blows were not undecided and ineffectual – lumbering like Mr Wordsworth's epic poetry, nor wavering like Mr Coleridge's lyric prose, nor short of the mark like Mr Brougham's speeches, nor wide of it like Mr Canning's wit, nor foul like the *Quarterly*, nor *let* balls like the *Edinburgh Review*.

They lose a little after a lapse of time.

> 4. Fortune is like the market, where many times, if you can stay a little, the price will fall; and again, it is sometimes like Sybilla's offer, which at first offereth the commodity at full, then consumeth part and part, and still holdeth up the price. – Bacon.

These are two direct and elaborated similes, the second depending for its effect on the reader's knowledge of Classical mythology, and therefore more appropriate to an age where such knowledge was more common than it is in our own. It reminds us of the fact that fashions in similes change, like fashions in words. Today, even such a stock simile or pseudo-simile as 'He was as rich as Croesus' requires some annotation.

> 5. Methinks I see in my mind a noble and puissant Nation rising like a strong man after sleep, and shaking her invincible locks. Methinks I see her as an Eagle mewing her mighty youth, and kindling her undazzled eyes at the full midday beam, purging and unscaling her long abused sight at the fountain itself of heavenly radiance, while the whole noise of timorous and flocking birds, with those that love the twilight, flutter about, amazed at what she means, and in their envious gabble would prognosticate a year of sects and schisms. – Milton.

This is, perhaps, the most famous simile in English prose. It has some outward affinities with, but is not, in fact, a Homeric simile, since it is not developed for its own sake, but in its cumulative detail is all the time closely related to the two elements of original and image – the 'puissant Nation' and the Eagle or, more simply, the strong man. Without its elaboration it would fail of its effect. Not, indeed, that a simile need be elaborated to have a kind of reverberating effect through the sentence. There is an example of this in the sentence of Landor already quoted (p. 12) where we cannot mentally dissociate Past, Present, and Future from the 'note in music'.

6. The west side of every wood and rising ground gleamed like a boundary of Elysium, and the sun on our backs seemed like a gentle herdsman driving us home at evening. – Thoreau.

The second of the two similes is peculiarly apt and evocative, and is heightened in effect by the use of the epithet *gentle*, with its suggestion of the setting, and therefore no longer dazzling or scorching, sun. The first, with its faintly Classical flavour and a certain abstractness, is more literary and artificial.

7. The cawing of rooks was not unlike the cry of a pack of hounds in hollow echoing woods, or the rushing of the wind in tall trees, or the tumbling of the tide upon a pebbly shore. – Gilbert White.

Here the writer is driven to simile. He is trying to describe a particular sound, and can do it only by reference to other sounds. It is to be noted that the epithets inside the similes – *hollow echoing*, *tall*, *pebbly* – are not idly picturesque but significant. They define the conditions under which the parallel sounds are heard. These similes, effectively piled up, separate, yet making a single whole, owe much of their effectiveness to detail.

So in the following sentence from Dryden, the first simile is rescued from triteness by the epithet *distant*, and the second, which is more original and unexpected, is in itself definite and precise:

8. And then, every one favouring his own curiosity with strict silence, it was not long ere they perceived the Air break about them like the noise of distant Thunder, or of swallows in a Chimney.

9. A very old man, bent but active, with white moustaches that bristled forward like those of a prawn, pushed open the swing door and went in. – George Orwell.

Prawn is the effective word. We are not concerned with the fact that the writer, forgetting or not knowing the name for the prawn's whiskery appendages, credits it with moustaches.

There is a little leap in, or concentration of, sense; just as there is a concentration of simile into metaphor in the familiar phrase 'walrus moustache'. This type of simile, which has the effect of giving a snapshot picture, is a familiar one with novelists in introducing their characters; as when Dickens says that Uncle Pumblechook had a 'mouth like a fish', or Hardy describes Gabriel Oak's wrinkles as 'extending upon his countenance like the rays in a rudimentary sketch of the rising sun'.

10. The pale-green sea curdled on the shingle and the green tower of the Metropole looked like a dug-up coin verdigrised with age-old mould. – Graham Greene.

Anybody who has been to Brighton and seen the Metropole Hotel will recognize the truth of this simile, which has at least a geographical parallel with the more indirect one of Sydney Smith concerning the Pavilion – that it looked as if Saint Paul's had come to Brighton and littered. But the simile does not go the whole way; it is applicable to colour only, not shape. In much modern writing, of which this is an example, there is a tendency for the simile to startle the reader with an element of surprise. Two simple examples from the same book (*Brighton Rock*) will illustrate this:

11. He wore a grey double-breasted waistcoat, and his eyes gleamed like raisins.

12. . . . his great teeth gleaming like an advertisement.

The words *raisins* and *advertisement* come unexpectedly, their association with *gleaming* is not obviously apparent. As in much modern use of metaphor, especially in poetry, there are undertones of meaning which the reader can appreciate only by some effort of imagination.

13. I was interrupted in my meditations by a noise like the Scotch express going under a bridge. It was Honoria Glossop laughing. – P. G. Wodehouse.

Hilaire Belloc once described Mr Wodehouse as one of the best modern writers of prose. Certainly he is a master, not only of a peculiarly expressive vocabulary and idiom, but also of the humorous simile which depends mainly on exaggeration. Here is another example – in form, a simile at the first remove. He is describing the noise made by a policeman falling through the roof of a conservatory:

14. I'm not nearly hot enough to draw a word-picture that would do justice to that extraordinarily hefty crash. Try to imagine the Albert Hall falling on the Crystal Palace, and you will have got the rough idea.

In the following passage the writer makes a statement and afterwards explains it by a simile:

15. If the mind be possessed with any Lust or Passions a man had better be in a Fair than in a Wood alone. They may, like petty Thieves, cheat us perhaps, and pick our pockets in the midst of company, but like Robbers they use [= are accustomed] to strip and bind, or murder us when we are alone. – Cowley.

Without the simile the statement is puzzling; but with it the contrast between being in a wood and being in a fair becomes apparent. The petty thief frequents the crowds, the robber prefers the lonely place. There is an imaginative reaction between statement and simile; one lights up and gives significance to the other.

Examples could, of course, be multiplied, but these will serve well enough to illustrate the use of the simile in various types of prose.

Simile is the starting-place or origin of metaphor. The step from one to the other is a short one. Metaphor gets rid of the sign: the two parts that make up the image merge into one by a kind of fusion. 'He needed not,' says Dryden of Shakespeare, 'the spectacles of books to read Nature.' That is a metaphor; it says in little what the simile would express in cumbrous periphrasis, 'He did not look at Nature through books as a man looks at a page of writing through a pair of spectacles'. Or we may catch the simile in the act of suggesting or illustrating a metaphor in its immediate context. Thus in this sentence from Addison, 'For these reasons the country gentleman, like the fox, never prowls near his own home', the metaphor implicit in the verb *prowls*, which is literally used of an animal, not a man, is suggested by and reflected in the simile 'like a fox'. The example is not a very apt or happy one, because *prowls* as used here is a dead or half-dead metaphor, its metaphorical having been assimilated to its literal sense. Here is a more pertinent one from De Quincey:

> The half-slumbering consciousness that many of these mails, like fire racing along a train of gunpowder, will be kindling at every instant new successions of burning joy, has an obscure effect of multiplying the victory itself.

The simile slips over into the two words *kindling* and *burning*; their metaphorical sense derives from the picture of the fire racing along the train of gunpowder.

This very passage reminds us that in prose the metaphor dwells most commonly in the single word. We are back in the realm of vocabulary. There is, as we have already noted, a continual traffic between literal and metaphorical meanings. It is at its briskest in speech; a little slower in writing, which trails upon the heels of speech. Over the range of literature we see changes of metaphorical use, as we see changes in spelling or syntax. For many words, especially derivatives from Greek and Latin, a modern dictionary gives the metaphorical as the accepted sense, with the literal meaning in a secondary place, marked *archaic* or *obsolete*. Thus the word *perplex*, from the Latin root *plicare* meaning 'weave', 'tangle', was once used literally. The *Shorter Oxford English Dictionary* has the quotation from Goldsmith, 'Now to perplex the ravell'd noose', and up to the eighteenth century it was possible to talk about 'a perplexed skein of wool'. But now the metaphorical – that is, the transferred – sense has triumphed. We speak of a 'perplexed mind', or by ellipsis a 'perplexed person', and of a 'perplexing question'. The original similes – a mind tangled like a piece of string, a question like a knot to be untied – are concentrated in a single word.

Metaphorical meaning develops, like other elements in the language, through the reaction of speech and writing. It goes without saying that its occurrence in literature is linked with the growth of the vocabulary; the modern writer having more words to draw upon has also a larger stock of metaphors, which are inherent in them. Today, for example, scores of words, reflecting the conditions of our own age, have acquired or are acquiring a metaphorical meaning in colloquial, including journalistic, usage, and await their acceptance into or their rejection from the more permanent language of literature.

So deeply, however, is metaphor entrenched in the vocabulary that we are scarcely conscious of it in the individual word. Indeed, many words are so commonly used out of their literal sense, that the mental picture they once suggested to both reader and writer is blurred and obscured; they are metaphorically dying or dead.[1] Thus when we read of 'the gravity of the situation' we are not conscious of that initial literary sense, 'weight', which we have when we speak of the 'force of gravity', by which an apple falls to ground or on the head of Isaac Newton. We may, indeed, keep the metaphor at least half alive by relating it to a word with similar metaphorical force – 'He was weighed down by the gravity of the situation'. But we may equally substitute for *weighed down* such a verb as *troubled* or *worried* without imperilling the sense or even weakening the effect of the sentence. The metaphor in the word is no longer alive and cannot affect the words associated with it; just as the metaphor in *perplex* (p. 51) is dead for the simple reason that the literal meaning is now forgotten. There is no suggestion that a dead metaphor – as it is implicit in an individual word – is any worse than a living one. Perhaps 'dead' is an unfortunate epithet, since the word itself goes on living in, as it were, another sphere. Only the living metaphor may be, and usually is, evocative; not – as the dead metaphor may still be – for its sound or form of subtle reverberations of meaning, but primarily for the image it calls up.

[1] For this see Fowler MEU s.v. metaphor.

This passing from life to death of verbal metaphor,[1] with all the intermediate stages of 'livingness', is itself a reminder that metaphor, 'figure of speech in which a name or descriptive term is transferred to some object different from, but analogous to, that to which it is properly applicable' (OED), is, in the phrase of Dr I. A. Richards, 'the omnipresent principle of language'. Metaphor is not 'a verbal matter, a shifting and displacement of words', but a natural outcome of thought, which 'proceeds by comparison, and the metaphors of language derive therefrom'.[2] In this primary, fundamental sense, therefore, we cannot and should not isolate it as a figure or an ornament. It is native to and part of all expression in speech and writing.

Nevertheless, metaphor may be a piece of deliberate and sustained imagery, though not so commonly in prose as in poetry. It occurs most often in that kind of prose which is rhetorical or verges on the poetic. Of this two examples will suffice, one (famous and familiar) from a writer of the past, the other from a writer of the present:

> I cannot praise a fugitive and cloistered virtue, unexercised and unbreathed, that never sallies out and sees her adversary, but slinks out of the race, where that immortal garland is to be run for without dust and heat. –Milton.

> Of all the arts, Tragedy is the proudest, the most triumphant; for it builds its shining citadel in the very centre of the enemy's country, on the very summit of his highest mountain; from its impregnable watch-towers, his camps and arsenals, his columns and forts are all revealed. – Bertrand Russell.[3]

It is noticeable that in the Milton passage the metaphor shifts from one image to another, from the fight (*sallies out –*

[1] A convenient if somewhat misleading term for the metaphor 'implicit in the individual word'.

[2] The subject is treated by Partridge in *Usage and Abusage*, with detailed references to Dr Richards's *The Philosophy of Rhetoric*.

[3] Quoted in Bonamy Dobrée's *Modern Prose Style*, a book which is heartily recommended to the reader.

adversary) to the athletic race, and that it is foreshadowed by the metaphor implicit in the words *fugitive* (= taking to flight) and *cloistered*. But there is no confusion, as in mixed metaphor;[1] only a natural development of pictures, as in the Bertrand Russell passage there is a piling up of details in a single image.

The essence of a sustained metaphor is that it should be appropriate. It must have a natural, not a meretricious or artificial, effect in its context, and must 'proceed by comparison' from the thought itself. Sometimes, it may even be an important element in humorous writing. Again, Mr Wodehouse furnishes us with a couple of examples:

> His eyes came out of his head like a prawn's, and once more his moustache foamed up against his breakwater of a nose.

> I am implying nothing derogatory to your cousin Madeline when I say that the idea of being united to her in the bonds of holy wedlock is one that freezes the gizzard.

Ben Jonson, loosely equating simile and metaphor in a general term 'similitude', has a wise word to say on this matter of appropriateness:

> Metaphors far fet [fetched] hinder to be understood, and affected, lose their grace. Or when the person fetcheth his translations [*translatio*, 'carrying across', the literal Latin equivalent of the Greek *metaphora*] from a wrong place. As if a Privy Counsellor should at the Table take his *Metaphor* from a dicing-house, or Ordinary, for a Vintner's Vault; or a Justice of Peace draw his similitudes from the *Mathematicks*; or a Divine from a Bawdy-house or Taverns; or a Gentleman of *Northamptonshire*, *Warwickshire*, or the *Midland*, should fetch all his Illustrations to his county neighbours from shipping, and tell them of the main *sheet*, and the Boulin [bowline].

His examples are unconvincing – there is no valid reason why the justice should not take his metaphors from mathematics

[1] See *Good English*, p. 138.

or the Midlander from the sea – but his general meaning is
clear and pertinent.

I stopped short in the sentence quoted from Bertrand
Russell on p. 53. His metaphor goes on: 'within its walls
the free life continues, while the legions of Death and Pain
and Despair and all the servile captains of tyrant Fate,
afford the burghers of that dauntless city new spectacles of
beauty'. That reminds us that metaphor often shades off
into, and is an integral part of, personification. The giving of
personal attributes to an inanimate thing is a familiar element of word association, as when we speak of the face of
the earth or the eye of day. But the personification of ab-
straction – an old device, common in all mythology – is in a
different category. It gives to 'airy nothings a local habitation and a name', and depends on a natural transference of
thought. Hope and Despair take on the features and are
invested with the powers of mankind, as Evil, in the person
of the Devil, is endowed with horns and a tail. We meet it
most commonly in poetry':

> Youth on the prow, and Pleasure at the helm.
> Fell Thirst and Famine scowl,
> A baleful smile upon their baffled guest.

'Personification', says Mr Day Lewis, 'is a cousin ger-
mane of the pathetic fallacy;[1] the latter gives life to the
inanimate or sympathy to the brute creation, the former
gives breath to the abstract.' He quotes from Mr W. H.
Auden a short passage in which there is 'a loosening up and
enlivening of the stiffest, most formal of imaging devices':

[1] A term coined by Ruskin, signifying the common figure or device
in literature by which the natural world is depicted as in sympathy with
the human emotions and passions. Thus:

> So saying, her rash hand in evil hour
> Forth reaching to the Fruit, she pluck'd, she eat:
> Earth felt the wound, and Nature from her seat
> Sighing through all her Works gave signs of woe
> That all was lost —
>
> Paradise Lost, ix, 780–4.

. . . those clearings where the shy humiliations
Gambol on sunny afternoons, the waterhole to which
The scarred rogue sorrow comes quickly in the small hours.

With that he contrasts unfavourably an earlier example, from Marvell:

> *My life is of a birth as rare*
> *As 'tis for object strange and high:*
> *It was begotten by despair*
> *Upon impossibility,*

lines which, he says, 'present only the faintest image'. The judgement is an odd one. It entirely ignores the fact that one important element in personification is a kind of epigrammatic conciseness. To me, at any rate, the Marvell lines

> *It was begotten by despair*
> *Upon impossibility,*

are poetically and figuratively charged in a way that the more diffuse image of Auden is not.

In prose personification is less common, except in so far as it follows the ordinary pattern of metaphor. Ordinarily, it is sustained, broadened, and heightened into allegory, 'other speech', as in *The Pilgrim's Progress*. But allegory goes a little farther than what may be called abstract personification. Faithful, Talkative, Giant Despair, and Mr Facing-both-ways are something more than personifications of Faith, Garrulity, Despair, and Hypocrisy; they stray from the realm of metaphor proper into the streets of Bedford. In other ways, too, allegory is not confined to personification proper. The symbolism has a wider range, it extends from the pilgrims themselves to the topography of their journey – the Hill Difficulty, with its two seductive by-passes, the ways called Destruction and Danger; the Valley of Humiliation and the Valley of the Shadow of Death; the Enchanted Ground and the Land of Beulah. Whenever a man writes in parables, clothing truth, as Bunyan himself says, 'in mantles', the imagery is sustained and diffused throughout the texture of his prose. Even so ordinarily 'prosaic' a writer as Addison sometimes drops into allegory:

> The Valley that thou seest, said he, is the Vale of Misery, and the Tide of Water that thou seest is part of the great Tide of Eternity . . . Examine now, said he, this Sea that is thus bounded with Darkness at both Ends, and tell me what thou discoverest in it. I see a Bridge, said I, standing in the midst of the Tide. The Bridge thou seest, said he, is humane [human] Life, consider it attentively.

As in the familiar parables of the New Testament, or the account of the Fall of Man in the Book of Genesis, elemental moral and spiritual principles are presented visually, with the detail and colour of a picture.

There is an element of personification at one remove, in the novel where the characters are 'flat' rather than 'round'. 'Flat characters', says Mr E. M. Forster in *Aspects of the Novel*, 'were called "humours" in the seventeenth century' – Shakespeare's Fluellen and Pistol are examples of them. At their simplest and most obvious we meet them in the romances of T. L. Peacock, *Crotchet Castle*, *Headlong Hall*, and the rest, which are, indeed, allegorical satires. Their names, a little disguised, are indicative of their characters – Dr Folliott, Mr Crotchet, Mr Milestone, Mr Listless, Mr Nightshade. So, too, though less obviously, are many of the names in Scott, Trollope, and especially Dickens. The subject of personal names in the novel is one that deserves a book on its own; and in such a book allegorical invention would have an important and significant place. A remote but suggestive personification is often present in the names of 'round' characters, those, that is, which have complexity and development within the story. Such names, for example, as Gabriel Oak, Giles Winterbourne, Eustacia Vye, Marty South, in the *Wessex Novels* have in themselves something of symbolism. When we meet them first on the page, they foreshadow the characters which are to reveal themselves as the plot unfolds.

But in particular metaphor is linked with idiom, the kind

of terse image that is suggested most often by the ordinary and familiar occupations of men, and passes, like colloquial and certain slang words, from common speech into the standard or literary language. Idioms are, in fact, crystallized metaphors, derived from the language of the housewife, the farmer, the soldier, the sailor, the sportsman, the artisan, the engineer. When they are first coined they belong to the private speech or jargon of the particular trade or profession in which they originated. Some, having a specialized significance, remain there; others, bandied about in ordinary conversation, move from one occupation to another and finally become the property of us all. An idiom, once current in speech or established in the literary language, is an entity like a word. It has a fixed form, and a 'properness' to the context, though it cannot normally have nuances of meaning. So, too, like words, idioms reflect life. A particular idiom comes into the language at a certain period in its history, a kind of verbal token of the human activities of that period. It follows that as the language develops it becomes richer in idioms as it becomes richer in words. We shall not find in eighteenth-century prose idioms that derived from the industrial or machine age that followed; nor in the prose of the nineteenth century those which belong to the motor car, the aeroplane, and the colloquial language of the First World War; nor in the period immediately before 1939 many that we owe to the growing influence of American speech and literature, and those that arise from the new political, social, and scientific pattern of what we are beginning to call the atomic age.

In brief, idioms are an integral part of the living texture of language. Some die as they grow remote from life; others, once alive, linger on in a kind of living death – mere clichés or stereotypes that have lost their force through long custom and conventional use. True living idioms are a heritage (sometimes in the form of proverbs, the folk-lore of language) bequeathed to the creative writer by ordinary men, metaphors ready made. Paradoxically they may also be killed by the same ordinary men, when they use them indiscriminately and insensitively. But it is a characteristic of those who write literature, memorable prose, that they know when an idiom is dead, and accordingly pass it by, as they pass by a word which, in Shakespeare's phrase, 'is over-worn'. All literature is, in the broad sense, idiomatic – whether the idiom belongs to syntax or to metaphor. It is in this that its living quality lies, a quality that ultimately relates it to the vitality of speech; and according as it lacks that quality, becoming what we sometimes term 'literary', it falls below the best.

Simile and metaphor, with their associates personification and allegory, are the basic figures of imagery in both prose and poetry. School text-books and school examinations make great play with others, like metonymy and synec-doche, in which individual words are given an associated meaning or extended function, as when we say 'a ruling from the chair' (metonymy), where the chair stands for or symbolizes the authority of the chairman, the person in charge of a meeting, or 'The factory employed three hundred hands' (synecdoche), where a part (*hands*) represents the whole. But these are no more than natural artifices of voca-bulary that are common in all speech and writing. They call for no special comment here. Devices like antithesis, climax, and paradox are treated as they arise in the chapter (VII) on Style. Of two of such devices, hyperbole and euphemism, however, a word must be said. In its extended or sustained form, hyperbole – deliberate exaggeration for effect – is more familiar in poetry than in prose. There is a notable example in *Hamlet* (v. 1, 273–5), and, in prose, at the end of the Gospel according to St John:

> And there are also many other things which Jesus did, the which, if they should be written every one, I suppose that even the world itself could not contain the books that should be written.

But the hyperbolical use of individual words is common in colloquial modern English – 'an *awful* shame', 'I'm *terribly* tired', 'It is a *tremendous* pity', 'a *fearful* mistake'.

Literature eschews such usages, except, of course, in its representations of ordinary speech, as in the novel and the play. It is interesting to note, however, that in eighteenth-century prose two such adjectives, *prodigious* and *vast*, with their corresponding adverbs, were often used with hyperbolical effect. 'As the news of my arrival spread through the kingdom,' says Gulliver, 'it brought prodigious numbers of rich, idle, and curious people to see me.' So Gilbert White writes of 'such prodigious flocks of birds', 'prodigious torrents', and 'vast drops of rain'. The adverbs *prodigiously* and *vastly* frequently occur in recorded conversation – 'I am prodigiously (or vastly) surprised'. Indeed, the phrase 'I shall be vastly surprised' still survives, somewhat precariously, and with a faint archaic literary flavour, in written English today.

Of euphemism, 'pleasant or decorous speech', there is only this to be said, that it is a special characteristic of Victorian literature, reflecting a mental or moral way of life in which it was indecorous to speak openly of the legs of a table, and of which the very word *unmentionables* is a revealing symbol. Before that, especially in the novel and the play, literature was sufficiently outspoken, and writers during the present century are certainly not backward in calling a spade a spade. Today, certainly, it is out of fashion. The old taboos have gone; and though from time to time a book comes under the law for containing especially sexual terms, there is in general an emphasis of what is itself somewhat euphemistically called realism, and a use – often harsh and unnecessary – of words that never passed beyond the bounds of the smoking-room. In all this there is both loss and gain – loss in that a frank vocabulary has become something of a cult which, in a subtle way, affects the normal verbal texture of both prose and verse; gain in that it facilitates a new directness of expression no longer tied to paraphrastic and often absurd innuendo.

But no study of figure and imagery can be complete without some reference to the work that has been done in recent years on semantics, 'the branch of philology concerned with meanings'. It is evident to us all that all words (except, for the purpose of this argument, pronouns and connectives) are complex; that is, as the etymology suggests (Latin *plectere*, 'plait') they are, as it were, folded into intricate patterns, not flat like a plane surface. To put it more simply, most nouns, verbs, and adjectives have in addition to their primary meaning various associated meanings. As far as it concerns the choice of words in writing, this elementary fact is touched upon in the chapter on Vocabulary (pp. 22 ff.). But the philosophy of meaning takes us much further. It has been enunciated in three notable English books – *The Meaning of Meaning*, by I. A. Richards and C. K. Ogden, and William Empson's two books (both inspired by Richards), *Seven Types of Ambiguity* and *The Study of Complex Words*. These go far beyond the range of the present book; indeed, they advance certain theories which cannot but bewilder the ordinary reader, and reach conclusions that seem, to me at any rate, strained and exaggerated. But it will be profitable at this point to follow them a little way, with Empson's *Seven Types* as the starting point.

'An ambiguity,' he says, ' in ordinary speech, means something very pronounced, and as a rule witty or deceitful. I propose to use the word in an extended sense, and shall think relevant to my subject any consequence of language, however slight, which adds some nuance to the direct statement of prose.' His book, as that statement implies, concerns poetry; and the reference to prose is significant since it suggests the general principle that, at any rate in expository prose, a word, though it of course retains its sense associations, has according to the context a single direct meaning, without nuance. That is not so true of imaginative prose – in the novel or the play; for the simple reason that such prose has certain of the characteristics of poetry. In the kind of ambiguity that Mr Empson has in mind there are related extensions of meaning either in a single word or in the effect produced by the juxtaposition of words; and these are always, or nearly always, bound up with figure and imagery. Thus he quotes Sir Herbert Read on metaphor:

'Metaphor is the synthesis of several units of observation into one commanding image; it is the expression of a complex idea, not by analysis, nor by direct statement, but by a sudden perception of an objective relation';[1]

and adds the comment: 'Thus I should call it an ambiguity when one thing is said to be like another, and they have several different properties in virtue of which they are alike ... I shall take this as normal to the simplest type of ambiguity.' The very word *metaphor* implies change, and in any consideration of the complexities of meaning it must have an important place, since (I quote Mr Empson again) it 'is the normal mode of development of a language'.

However, for a single and comparatively straightforward example we will go to Mr Empson's third ambiguity. He defines it thus: 'An ambiguity of the third type, considered as a verbal matter, occurs when two ideas, which are connected only by being both relevant in the context, can be given in one word simultaneously.' In simple language it is the pun, or, extending the significance a little *paronomasia*, a play on words. Of this ambiguity the pun which depends on verbal cleverness, often an accidental relationship of sound, is a superficial manifestation. It is familiar to us in Shakespeare:

> Not on thy sole but on thy soul, harsh Jew,
> Thou makest thy knife keen
>
> O world! thou wast the forest to this hart;
> And this, indeed, O world! the heart of thee.

There was, too, a notable outbreak of punning in the early nineteenth century. One of Charles Lamb's puns will suffice for illustration; it is recorded by Crabb Robinson in his *Diary* (June 13, 1811): 'The large room in the accountant's office in the East India House is divided into boxes or divisions in each of which sit six clerks (Charles Lamb himself is one). They are called *compounds*. The meaning of the word was asked one there. Lamb said it was evident – "A

[1] *English Prose Style.*

collection of simples".' In verse, Thomas Hood played on
words with amazing ingenuity:

> '*O Sally Brown, O Sally Brown,*
>   *How could you serve me so?*
> *I've met with many a breeze before,*
>   *But never such a blow:*'

> *Then reading on his 'bacco box*
>   *He heaved a bitter sigh,*
> *And then began to eye his pipe,*
>   *And then to pipe his eye.*

> *His death, which happen'd in his berth,*
>   *At forty-odd befell:*
> *They went and told the sexton, and*
>   *The sexton toll'd the bell.*

But paronomasia ('equal word') can be and often is more
subtle. It is a common figure that sets up thought associations, and intensifies or illuminates meaning, by a certain
imaginative but often unconscious trickery with words
themselves; and, like euphemism (to which in certain ways it
is allied) it is deep-rooted. Oddly enough, there are several
examples in the Bible, though they are disguised in our English translation. Thus in the passage from the prophet Amos:
'And he said, Amos, what seest thou? And I said, A basket
of summer fruit. Then said the Lord unto me, The end is
come upon my people Israel', the sense and significance lies
in the punning juxtaposition of the two Hebrew words *kayis*
(summer fruit) and *kes* (end). So in his letter to Philemon
Paul puns upon the name (*Onesimus* = 'profitable') of the
runaway slave, 'which in time past was to thee unprofitable,
but now profitable to thee and to me', just as, indeed, Christ
Himself punned upon the name Peter (*Petros*) in the phrase
'upon this rock (*petra*) I will build my church'.

There are plenty of examples, too, in our own literature.
Two will suffice, one from an old and one from a modern

poet. The first is from Milton's *On the Morning of Christ's Nativity*:

> *The Sun himself with-held his wonted speed,*
> *And hid his head for shame,*
> *As his inferiour flame,*
> *The new enlightn'd world no more should need;*
> *He saw a greater Sun appear*
> *Then his bright Throne, or burning Axletree could bear.*

Milton wrote *Sun* in both the first and the fifth line; and the simple, direct meaning is perfectly clear. But in the fifth line an ambiguity arises from the sound of the word. *Sun* is here metaphorical, following on from the literal *Sun* a line or two before; but it also suggests *Son*, especially if we happen to know that *Sun* was often spelt *Sonne* in Milton's time. The association of thought is helped by what seems to be an accidental association of words.

The second is from the poem of Henry Reed which is mentioned on page 197:

> *And this you can see is the bolt. The purpose of this*
> *Is to open the breech, as you see. We can slide it*
> *Rapidly backwards and forwards: we call this*
> *Easing the spring. And rapidly backwards and forwards*
> *The early bees are assaulting and fumbling the flowers:*
> > *They call it easing the Spring.*

There the pun is deliberate – the play upon the spring of the rifle and Spring the season. But it is not a mere piece of verbal ingenuity, a clever joke. The two sentences express two ideas that are at once parallel and contrasted. So the language in one echoes the language in the other, emphasizing both the parallelism and the contrast; and this device of repetitive echo – a very common one in modern verse – is rounded off by the actual punning echo in the last word of each sentence (*spring – Spring*).

Mr Empson himself is alert to far greater subtleties than this. How far he can press this type of ambiguity may be illustrated from his note on a line from *Samson Agonistes*, where Samson is speaking of Dalila:

> *That specious monster, my accomplished snare.*

Here, he says, we have an ambiguity that is effected 'by reference to derivation'; and he goes on to explain:

> *Specious*, 'beautiful and deceitful'; *monster*, 'something unnatural and something striking shown as a sign of disaster'; *accomplished*, 'skilled in the arts of blandishment and successful in undoing her husband'. The point here is the sharpness of distinction between the two meanings, of which the reader is forced to be aware; they are two pieces of information, two parts of the narrative; if ingenuity had not used an accident, they would have required two words.

'Of which the reader is forced to be aware' seems to be something of an assumption; and, indeed, the reader of Mr Empson is often tempted to cry, with Horatio, ' 'Twere to consider too curiously to consider so'.

And readers not only of Mr Empson but also of many other critics who make something of a cult of poetic imagery, imagining in it all kinds of hidden significances that probably the poet himself never dreamed of and did not intend; as, for example, Mr Day Lewis, who quotes Mr Auden's lines

> *O dear white children, casual as birds,*
> *Playing amid the ruined languages,*

and declares that from the word *white* his mind 'received an image of white doves, pecking about at the foot of broken columns white in sunlight', and says of three other short passages in which the same epithet appears, including A. E. Housman's

> *White in the moon the long road lies*
> *That leads me from my love,*

that in each of them the image (of whiteness) 'means separation, from love or from youth'. Admittedly, Mr Auden's meaning is open to almost any interpretation the reader may care to put upon it; but that only argues a certain lack of precision rather than an abundance of imagination in the poet himself. As for the Housman passage, it is arguable that *white* is not figurative at all, but literal. Mr Lewis, in the modern manner, has found a significance of imagery where there is neither imagery nor figurative significance. The truer interpretation is that out of a number of literal monosyllabic epithets Housman, with his unfailing sense of the exact word, used the one which was most poetically apt and effective. More prosaically, in those dusty days of the late 1890's the road probably was white. Housman was merely stating the simple truth.

But the analytic semantic approach does make us aware of the potency of the individual word, and the subtle extensions of meaning from the literal to the figurative. It explains how words, having such ambiguities, are often used especially by poets in relationships that depend upon their ambiguities (in, of course, the Empsonian sense), not upon conventional meaning or conventional syntax. Communication between poet and reader is not, and is not meant to be, complete, as it is (normally) in expository prose. The latent image in one word is reflected in the latent image in another. There can be no ordinary prosaic equivalent or paraphrase, because all the 'meaning' depends upon evocatives that are occasioned by the words themselves. In much modern poetry the old landmarks of subject and predicate, clause and phrase, and often punctuation no longer exist because the 'meaning' – or better, the poetic effect – is in the sensations occasioned by the words themselves.

However, as long as the gap between the private mind of the writer (especially the poet) and the reader is not too wide – that is, as long as there is some recognizable process of intelligible communication – the semantic analysis helps to make plain, or at any rate plainer what else would be obscure. But, especially in respect of the older 'conventional' poets, it has the disadvantage that it sometimes tends to make obscure what to the ordinary reader, not possessed by (or of) seven ambiguities, is perfectly and pleasantly plain. Even Mr Robert Graves, the apostle of modernist poetry in the true sense, is troubled on this score. 'When,' he says, 'modernist poetry, or what not so long ago passed for modernist poetry, can reach the stage where the following piece by Mr Ezra Pound:

> Papyrus
> *Spring* . . .
> *Too long* . . .
> *Gongula* . . .

is seriously offered as a poem, there is some justification for the plain reader and orthodox critic who shrinks from anything that may be labelled "modernist" either in terms of condemnation or approbation.' To the plain reader and orthodox critics these are comforting and reassuring words.

CHAPTER IV

A NOTE ON QUOTATION AND ALLUSION

'Yes, sir. Smethurst – his name is Smethurst – would consider it a consummation devoutly to be wished.'
'Rather well put, that, Jeeves. Your own?'
'No, sir. The Swan of Avon, sir.'

MUCH OF our metaphorical idiom arises, as we have seen, in the common speech. But it is equally true that the written word, literature, creates its own heritage, not necessarily of idioms, but of memorable phrases that pass into the language; in other words, a writer may strike out a phrase or a sentence that by its vividness or evocative quality becomes the property of succeeding writers, who use it as they would use an ordinary idiom, sometimes even without the acknowledgement of quotation marks. Mr C. E. Montague argues that the man who reads few books with true and abiding enjoyment is the best and most natural quoter. 'The only mental food,' he says, 'that will turn to new tissue within you, and build itself into your mind, is that which you eat with a good surge of joy and surprise that anything so exciting should ever have been written.' In the course of the chapter he illustrates his point: 'You can turn author yourself. You can go tend the homely, slighted shepherd's trade.' Out of his reading of Milton (*Lycidas*, 1, 65) he remembers a striking phrase – which has, in fact, passed into general use – and weaves it into the texture of his own prose. 'That's rather well put, Montague,' Bertie Wooster would have said. 'Your own?'

What C. E. Montague does we all do, even in our speech, according to our memory and the extent of our reading – according, that is, as we have our minds stored with prose and poetry. '*Hamlet*,' a lady is reported to have said, 'is all quotations.' It is, in a general exaggerated way, true. 'To the

manner born', 'in my mind's eye', 'more honoured in the
breach than the observance', 'hoist with his own petard' –
these and many others are part of our own stock-in-trade,
ready for the lip or for the pen, even if we are not aware
when we speak or write of their origin. They are, as Lamb
said of certain books, 'great Nature's stereotypes'. The
Shakespeare plays are full of them. So, above all, is the
Bible: 'corn in Egypt', 'the valley of the shadow of death',
'by the skin of my teeth', 'the old Adam', 'kill the fatted
calf', 'in the twinkling of an eye', 'the new Jerusalem' –
these few, out of hundreds, casually remembered as I wrote
this sentence. Most writers, especially poets, make their
contribution. When we write or say 'this side idolatry' we
are quoting from Ben Jonson, 'give hostages to fortune'
from Bacon, 'here is God's plenty' from Dryden, 'To travel
hopefully is a better thing than to arrive' from R. L. Stevenson, 'the still sad music of humanity' from Wordsworth, 'a
sadder and a wiser man' from Coleridge, 'Beauty is Truth'
from Keats, ''Tis better to have loved and lost' from
Tennyson, 'the coloured counties' from A. E. Housman,
'their finest hour' from Sir Winston Churchill. Again I have
quoted as the phrases occurred to me, without reference to
books; they happen to be, in another phrase of Montague's,
'comfortably within reach of my hand'. But for the truly
well-read man the treasure is almost inexhaustible; 'the line'
(to drift at once into quotation and hyperbole) 'stretches
out to the crack of doom'. It is by this transmuting power,
which turns to gold certain collocations of words, whether
in prose or poetry, that great writers repay, with magnificent
interest, their debt to the language they use.

They pay their debt, let us remind ourselves, unconsciously; they are not aware that this phrase or that is going
to take upon itself a peculiar quality of permanence. But the
quoter's art is a conscious one; he knows he is handling the
bequeathed riches of other men. He therefore has his
responsibilities. For quotation, like the use of metaphor and
idiom, has to conform to certain principles – in particular,
the basic principle of aptness. It follows an original thought,

and sets a seal upon it. Though it is common property,
known and read of all men, it must retain in its new context freshness and originality. It is a sad truth that quotations, even (and perhaps especially) the choicest of them,
may be dulled by use, and become the worse for wear.
Nevertheless the context can revivify them and make them
shine again in something of their original splendour. The
truly apt quotation lights up – in the literal sense *illustrates*
– the sentence or passage of which it forms a part; and, as if
in return, a kind of reflected light shines back upon the
quotation. Author and quoter work together. When (to take
an example at random) we read in Hazlitt 'The designing
knave may sometimes wear a vizor, or, "to beguile the
time, look like the time", but watch him narrowly, and you
will detect him behind his mask', we are conscious that
Shakespeare[1] and Hazlitt are in collaboration; the whole
sentence is Hazlitt's, but it owes something of its effectiveness to the hand of Shakespeare.

Spontaneous quotation – that is, the quotation of remembered things – is not, in fact, common in our early prose.
Where it does occur, ten to one it is drawn from the classical
languages. There is a familiar instance in Dryden's eulogy
of Shakespeare:

> But he is always great when some great occasion is pre-
> sented to him; no man can say he ever had a fit subject
> for his wit and did not then raise himself as high above the
> rest of the poets,
> *Quantum lenta solent inter viburna cupressi*[2]

That may be remembered (we cannot tell); at any rate, we
feel that it was on the threshold of Dryden's mind, that he
had not to search for it. Quotations of this kind, mainly
from Latin verse, abound in such works as Sidney's *Apologie
for Poetrie*, and in Bacon's and Cowley's *Essays*. The reason
is fairly obvious. Up to the early eighteenth century the
great Classical tradition held sway. English itself was re-
garded as scarcely a worthy language to quote from; and

[1] *Macbeth* 1, v, 64–5.   [2] Virgil, *Eclogues* 1, 26.

in any case the early writers had only a comparatively small body of literature from which to quote. Modern critics and essayists have a far wider field to explore either in memory, or by actual deliberate reference to books; and they turn, for the most part, to the poets, or less frequently the prose writers, of their own language.

In an essay written some twenty years ago the late James Agate accused C. E. Montague himself of being 'a lugger-in of quotations'. The accusation, which has some smack of truth in it, is a reminder that quotation can be overdone. Over-quotation affects some writers like a disease. Hazlitt had a touch of it. Turn, for example, the pages of his essay *On the Fear of Death*. It is prefaced with the obvious quotation from *The Tempest*. 'And our little life is rounded with a sleep', and there are in the body of the essay about twenty illustrative passages from prose and poetry, duly acknowledged by inverted commas, as well as several others which are, as it were, embedded in his sentences without acknowledgement, and one longish passage in prose which he deliberately introduces to elaborate a statement of his own. It would be untrue to say that the twenty illustrative quotations spoil the essay; Hazlitt is too good a writer for that. But they tend to overweight it a little. The Hazlitt who goes on a journey 'repeating lines from Mr Coleridge's poems' is too uncomfortably present. He pauses a trifle too often in his prose, if not in his walk, to draw upon the stores of his well-filled mind, and remind us of the poverty of our own.[1] Lamb, too, is an inveterate quoter in the *Essays*, as he was punster in his conversation and journalistic bagatelles; and his quotations are, in the main, more evocative than Hazlitt's, as when speaking of the 'distant correspondent' Bernard Manning he says:

> But while I talk, I think you hear me, – thoughts dallying with vain surmise –

[1] Such quotation sometimes becomes an irritating affectation, as in the Lord Peter Wimsey stories of Miss Dorothy Sayers (e.g. *Busman's Honeymoon*).

*Aye me! while thee the seas and sounding shores
Hold far away.*[1]

The *Essays of Elia* abound in phrases and passages of that kind which Lamb remembered out of his vast reading of, and love for, the older prose writers and poets. It is, indeed, not too much to say that illustrative quotation is one of the outstanding characteristics of his individual and peculiar style.

I have already spoken of Hazlitt's 'embedded quotations' – that is, those which – often a little altered or modified – are not introduced, as it were, from outside, but are assimilated into his own prose. They are allusive rather than illustrative, what James Agate in the essay already quoted calls 'buried references'. Their effect is not to present us directly with another writer's phrase but to set up an echo of it in the mind:

I neither ate, drank, nor was merry, yet I did not complain.

Or do ye complain that pain no longer visits you, that sickness has done its worst.

The first derives from the Bible, 'Take thine ease, eat, drink, and be merry' (Luke, xii, 19); the second is adapted from *Macbeth*, 'Treason has done its worst' (iii, 2, 24). Hazlitt takes the original and moulds it to his own fashion, fitting it to his context, which thus becomes richer with the wealth of other literature. So, in varying measure, do other writers. When, for example, Bacon writes, 'Some books are to be tasted, others to be swallowed, and some few to be chewed and digested', he was, we imagine, faintly remembering the phrase in the Prayer Book collect, 'that we may in such wise hear them [the Scriptures], read, mark, learn, and inwardly digest them'. There is a constant verbal reverberation in literature; out of his subconscious mind one writer echoes another by a kind of inspired and legitimate plagiarism. A mode of expression in writing becomes, to some extent, common property, like the idioms of speech.

[1] Milton, *Lycidas* 154–5.

Allusive quotation or adaptation is, as any assiduous annotator will demonstrate, as common in poetry as in prose. But it is sometimes, rather curiously, deliberate. Gray, for example, was at pains to show that in his two Pindaric Odes (*The Bard* and *The Progress of Poesy*) he was frequently quoting from, or adapting the lines of, others. He notes Shakespeare, Milton, Dryden, Cowley, Virgil, and several other poets as the originators of his own phrases and expressions. A striking example occurs in *The Bard* (1, 41):

> '*Dear, as the ruddy drops that warm my heart,*
> *Ye died amidst your dying country's cries*',

which is an echo, and indeed a little more than an echo, of Shakespeare's lines in *Julius Caesar* (ii, 1, 289–90):

> '*As dear to me as are the ruddy drops*
> *That visit this sad heart*'.

In our own times, mainly in the early work of Mr T. S. Eliot, especially *The Waste Land*, deliberate allusive quotation (often abstruse) is a poetic artifice. The second part ('A Game of Chess') for example, opens with a line lifted straight from Shakespeare, 'The chair she sat in, like a burnished throne', and includes another further on, 'Those are pearls that were his eyes'; and besides these there are several more from English and Classical sources, not directly quoted, but echoed allusively, all of which Mr Eliot, like Gray, obligingly records in notes. He uses them as he uses established idioms and words, as part of the common store of language, deeming that the recollected felicities of the past can be moulded into, and help to fashion, a poetic idiom of his own.

Closely allied to allusive quotation is allusion in the broad sense, to proper names or to episodes in mythology, history, or literature itself. Classical allusions, especially in Shakespeare, are old friends, or foes, of our schooldays. They permeate all our early literature, when the Classical tradition was strong. It is, I think, Sir Richard Livingstone who observes that, with the decline of Latin and Greek studies, the inward meaning and effect of much great writing is closed to the modern generation, as he proved by setting a test in allusion to a mixed group of university students. Only through the veil of annotation and the Classical dictionary can they see and understand, for example, the opening lines of the last act of *The Merchant of Venice* or this famous sentence from Sir Thomas Browne:

'What song the *Syrens* sang, or what name *Achilles* assumed when he hid himself among Women, though puzzling Questions, are not beyond all conjecture.'

What was once known and open to the ordinary intelligent reader now has to be laboriously explained. Still, the allusions are there, enriching and illuminating our prose and poetry; the fact that, through a change in educational emphasis and practice, we can no longer fully appreciate them at sight is rather our misfortune than our fault.

But in fact all allusion, which travels far beyond the limits of Classical mythology and ranges the whole world, is bound in the nature of things to leave the reader panting a little way behind. The writer, like the setter of a quiz or a crossword puzzle, has the advantage. His allusions may be drawn out of a common stock – the Bible, literature both ancient and modern, famous characters, the great events of history; and then the reader is, or ought to be, able to follow him, if only at a distance. But they may be more private to himself, the harvest of a deep or specialized learning; and then the reader can only follow afar off – often, indeed, loses him altogether. But this does not make writing abstruse or obscure; it simply means that the writer is possessed of certain knowledge that the reader does not possess. Allusions are an integral part of his thought and his matter. This is true of purely topical references, such as occur often in essays, which depend for their effect upon a purely temporal and transient appeal. These often pass us by, the writer forgot, or did not realize that he was writing for posterity. In brief, there is a sense in which the reader, not being omniscient, has to accept allusions in faith. He may fly to the notes or the reference book, and make a labour of love; or he may frankly recognize the fact that in this, as in other ways, there is a point past which he cannot go. For literature demands imagination in the reading as well as in the writing. Understanding, the comprehension of meaning, is not all.

Of the sustained quotation which is introduced to support the writer's argument or confirm and illustrate his statement little need be said. *Si monumentum requiris, circumspice* – there are plenty of examples in this book. In literature (as distinct from work-a-day prose such as this) it naturally belongs, first and foremost, to criticism and biography. The writer says in effect, 'This or that is characteristic of the poet's or the novelist's style, and here is a passage to prove it'; or 'Here is something from another writer to elucidate that point'; or 'This man was accustomed to think or act in such and such a way, as you will see from this excerpt from one of his books or letters'. One example will suffice, taken almost at random. Mr T. S. Eliot in a lecture on Milton has turned aside to say something about blank verse, and breaks off to call Dr Johnson as a witness:

It is interesting at this point to recall the general observations upon blank verse, which a consideration of *Paradise Lost* prompted Johnson to make towards the end of his essay.

The music of the English heroic lines strikes the ear so faintly, that it is easily lost, unless all the syllables of every line co-operate together; this co-operation can only be obtained by the preservation of every verse unmingled with another as a distinct system of sounds; and this distinctness is obtained and preserved by the artifice of rhyme. The variety of pauses, so much boasted by the lovers of blank verse, changes the measures of an English poet to the periods of a declaimer; and there are only a few skilful and happy readers of Milton, who enable their audience to perceive where the lines end or begin. Blank verse, said an ingenious critic, seems to be verse only to the eye.

Some of my audience may recall that this last remark, in almost the same words, was often made, a literary generation ago, about the 'free verse' of the period: and even without this encouragement from Johnson it would have occurred to my mind to declare Milton to be the greatest master of free verse in our language. What is interesting about Johnson's paragraph, however, is that it represents the judgement of a man who had by no means a deaf ear, but simply a *specialized* ear, for verbal music.

Like the illustrative and allusive quotation, it is apt to its context, purposefully relevant. It is a part of the sustained argument, not an element in the writer's style. Again the two writers, quoted and quoter, collaborate, but in a special way; the quotation is a kind of text, and the commentary upon it the sermon.

Finally, a word on misquotation. This is a venial sin we are all prone to, since memory is only too apt to turn traitor. But there is, as Malvolio said, 'reason for 't'. Just as the writer necessarily alters an allusive quotation and adapts it to his own context, so we sometimes take a liberty with a remembered phrase; or, more precisely, we imperfectly remember it because we are pressing it into our own immediate service. Even syntax may enter into the matter. We tend to say or write 'make assurance doubly sure', where Shakespeare wrote 'double sure', because we instinctively demand an adverb (*doubly*) for Shakespeare's adjective form (*double*). Or figure of speech may play its part. Milton wrote 'Tomorrow to fresh woods and pastures new'; we substitute *fields* because that word has an appropriate metaphorical sense. Or we may reshape a phrase merely for convenience; out of Shakespeare's 'Though this be madness, yet there is method in 't' we make 'There is method in his madness'. Nor is this habit confined to ordinary men. As it happens, an example has already been quoted from Charles Lamb on p. 72. The sentence in *Lycidas* runs:

> *Ay me! while thee the seas and sounding shores*
> Wash *far away.*

Milton was referring to the dead body of his friend, Edward King; Lamb, by substituting the word *hold*, relates it to the still-living Bernard Manning at the other end of the world. So Gilbert White, for his own purpose, consciously and deliberately changes an epithet:

> 'The note of the former [the black-cap] has such a wild sweetness that it always brings to my mind those lines in a song in *As You Like It*:
>
>> "*And tune his merry note*
>> *Unto the* wild *bird's throat*".'

He substitutes (and italicizes) *wild* for Shakespeare's *sweet* because it is apt to his own observation. It is curious that in literature the evocative effect of quotation is not spoilt, but may be heightened, when the quotation goes a little awry.

CHAPTER V

SPEECH IN LITERATURE

1

But first I pray yow, of your curteisye,
That ye n'arette it nat my vileinye,
Thogh that I pleynly speke in this matere,
To telle yow hir wordes and hir chere;
Ne thogh I speke hir wordes properly.
For this ye knowen al-so wel as I,
Who-so shal telle a tale after a man,
He moot reherce, as ny as ever he can,
Everich a word, if it be in his charge,
Al speke he never so rudeliche and large;
Or elles he moot telle his tale untrewe,
Or feyne thing, or finde wordes newe,
He may nat spare, al-thogh he were his brother;
He moot as wel seye o word as another.

THIS IS not only Chaucer's apology (through the mouth of
Harry Bailey, the Host) for certain broad and bawdy passages in the *Tales*, but also a brief manifesto of the rights,
privileges, and responsibilities of an author. When he records the conversation of another man, Chaucer declares,
he must repeat, as far as he can, 'every single word'. Otherwise he writes an untrue and feigning story. Chaucer himself, in certain passages, does not hesitate to practise what he
preaches; and even when his characters are not speaking
'rudeliche and large', their talk, allowing for the modifications necessitated by metre and rhyme, has the ring of truth
about it. Here is the drunken Shipman arguing with the
Host:

Our hoste up-on his stiropes stood anon,
And seyde, 'Good men, herkneth everich on;

78

This was a thrifty tale for the nones!
Sir parish prest,' quod he, 'for goddes bones,
Tel us a tale, as was thy forward yore.
I see wel that ye lerned men in lore
Can moche good, by goddes dignitee!'
  The Persone him answerde, 'Ben'cite!
What eyleth the man, so sinfully to swere?'
  Our hoste answerde, 'O Jankin, be ye there?
I smelle a loller in the wind,' quod he.
'How! good men,' quod our hoste, 'herkneth me;
Abydeth, for goddes digne passioun,
For we shal han a predicacioun;
This loller heer wil prechen us som-what.'
  'Nay, by my fader soule! that shal be nat,'
Seyde the Shipman; 'heer he shal nat preche,
He shal no gospel glosen heer ne teche.
We leve alle in the grete god,' quod he,
'He wolde sowen som difficultee,
Or springen cokkel in our clene corn;
And therfor, hoste, I warne thee biforn,
My joly body shal a tale telle,
And I shal clinken yow so mery a belle,
That I shal waken al this companye;
But it shal nat ben of philosophye,
Ne physices, ne termes queinte of lawe;
Ther is but litel Latin in my awe.'

'A thrifty tale for the nones', 'springen cokkel in our clene corn', 'my joly body', 'shal clinken yow so mery a belle' – these are the accents of speech, the kind of phrases which with their forcefulness and vividness give life to language, and have an impact on the written word. The poet becomes the reporter of things overheard, he speaks 'hir wordes properly', and they become part of his poetry.

Yet the fusion of colloquial and literary, in this direct and outward sense, is never truly absolute. 'As ny as ever he can', says Chaucer; and the expression is significant. For the transference of authentic speech to writing is rendered difficult not only because of defects in memory, but also because inevitably the writer himself takes a hand. But here a distinction must be made. Speech occurs in writing, in two ways – factually, as in biography and autobiography, including the diary and the journal, and imaginatively, in the novel, the play, and (less frequently) the poem. In the former, the writer purports to record a conversation which he has overheard or in which he has taken part; in the latter, he tries to catch the accent and idiom of familiar conversation and appropriate it to his characters. Theoretically, factual speech is real, though in practice, partly because the writer's memory fails him in detail, it is rarely, we may assume, reported *verbatim*; imaginative speech, depending upon something remembered not particularly but generally, is not so much transferred as transmuted by the writer's own inventive and creative thought. In both, the writer is an intermediary; he stands between the speaker and the reader. Literature, the written word, wears the spoken word, in Shakespeare's phrase, 'with a difference'. Three passages will illustrate this:

Many of them seemed to be a little surprised, and were sinking apace into seriousness, when their champion appeared, and coming close to me, asked by what authority I did these things.

I replied, 'By the authority of Jesus Christ, conveyed to me by the (now) Archbishop of Canterbury, when he laid hands upon me, and said, "Take thou authority to preach the Gospel".' He said, 'This is contrary to Act of Parliament: this is a conventicle.' I answered, 'Sir, the conventicles mentioned in that Act (as the preamble shows) are seditious meetings; but this is not such; here is no shadow of sedition; therefore it is not contrary to that Act.' He replied, 'I say it is: and, beside, your preaching frightens people out of their wits.'

'Sir, did you ever hear me preach?' 'No.' 'How, then, can you judge of what you have never heard?' 'Sir, by common report.' 'Common report is not enough. Give me leave, Sir, to ask, Is not your name Nash?' 'My name is Nash.' 'Sir, I dare not judge of you by common report: I think it not enough to judge by.' Here he paused awhile, and, having recovered himself, said, 'I desire to know what this people comes here for': on which one replied, 'Sir, leave him to me: let an old woman answer him. You, Mr Nash, take care of your body; we take care of our souls; and for the food of our souls we come here.' He replied not a word, but walked away.

Mrs Montague, a lady distinguished for having written an Essay on Shakespeare, being mentioned;

REYNOLDS: 'I think that essay does her honour.'

JOHNSON: 'Yes, Sir; it does *her* honour, but it would do nobody else honour. I have, indeed, not read it all. But when I take up the end of a web, and find it pack-thread, I do not expect, by looking further, to find embroidery. Sir, I will venture to say, there is not one sentence of true criticism in her book.'

GARRICK: 'But, Sir, surely it shows how much Voltaire has mistaken Shakespeare, which nobody else has done.'

JOHNSON: 'Sir, nobody else has thought it worth while. And what merit is there in that? You may as well praise a schoolmaster for whipping a boy who has construed ill. No, Sir, there is no real criticism in it: none shewing the beauty of thought, as formed on the workings of the human heart.' . . .

'Come, come!' said H——; 'I thought we should have no heroes, real or fabulous. What say you, Mr Lamb? Are you for eking out your shadowy list with such names as Alexander, Julius Caesar, Tamerlane, or Ghengis Khan?' 'Excuse me,' said Lamb, 'on the subject of characters in active life, plotters and disturbers of the world, I have a crotchet of my own, which I beg leave to reserve.' – 'No, no! come, out with your worthies!' – 'What do you think of Guy Fawkes and Judas Iscariot?' H—— turned an eye upon him like a wild Indian, but cordial and full of smothered glee. 'Your most exquisite reason!' was echoed on all sides; and A[yrton] thought that Lamb had now fairly entangled himself. 'Why I cannot but think,' retorted he of the wistful countenance, 'that Guy Fawkes, that poor, fluttering annual scarecrow of straw and rags, is an ill-used gentleman. I would give something to see him sitting pale and emaciated, surrounded by his matches and his barrels of gunpowder, and expecting the moment that was to transport him to Paradise for his heroic self-devotion; but if I say any more, there is that fellow G[odwin] will make something of it. And as to Judas Iscariot, my reason is different. I would fain see the face of him who, having dipped his hand in the same dish with the Son of Man, could afterwards betray him. I have no conception of such a thing; nor have I ever seen any picture (not even Leonardo's very fine one) that gave me the least idea of it.' – 'You have said enough, Mr Lamb, to justify your choice.'

The first passage is from one of the most unjustly neglected books in English literature, John Wesley's *Journal*. 'It is remarkable,' said Edward Fitzgerald, recommending it in a letter to a friend, 'to read pure, unaffected, and undying English, while Addison and Johnson are tainted with a style which all the world imitated!' That unaffectedness is apparent in the recorded conversation. We cannot, of course, be sure that these were the actual words which passed between Wesley and Beau Nash in Bath on the fifth of June 1739. No doubt there were hesitancies, repetitions, little breakings-off in the sentences as they were spoken. The record has been a little touched up in the writing. But it rings true. It has done no more than smooth out certain roughnesses; and the accents of speech are preserved.

With Boswell there is a difference, but only a difference of degree. He is recording the words of a man whom he himself has presented as the greatest English conversationalist. We know that he assiduously jotted down Johnson's talk at the time – Gray called him 'a fool with a note-book'; and we are safe in assuming that in general Johnson spoke as Boswell reports him. The metaphor of the web, the pack-thread, and the embroidery we may be sure is Johnson's, and the reference to the schoolmaster whipping a boy. All the same, Boswell was 'writing it up'. No doubt a word here and a phrase there assists the flow and rounds off the rhythm of the sentence. We are hearing Johnson at one remove; his speech comes to us by way of the pen of Boswell.

The Hazlitt passage is further removed from the actual. He is remembering, long afterwards, a conversation at Lamb's house; and we feel that he rather uses direct speech as a device than reproduces it as a record. He hovers, that is, between fact and fiction; for example, he deliberately confuses the initials of the speakers so as to give, according to the peculiar fashion of the period, an effect of whimsical mystification. The speech of Lamb and the others is inextricably bound up with the art, or artifice, of Hazlitt's essay. We are hearing them not at one remove, but at two or even three. The voice is the voice of Lamb, imperfectly recollected, but the hands are the hands of Hazlitt.

So we come, by a natural process, to fictional speech; and here we are at once in deeper water. We know, from the outset, that we are in truth listening to the writer, who, having created certain characters, speaks through them. It is Chaucer who strikes out the phrase 'springen cokkel in our clene corn', and puts it into the mouth of the shipman; we can only conjecture, with some confidence, that it is the kind of expression he had heard people use, that it belongs to the coinage of current speech. But we are equally confident that the shipman did not speak in measured syllables with rhyming endings. That is the poet's domain; he has wrested speech to his own conventions. True, the speech may itself be colloquial, as it is in Chaucer himself, or Crabbe, or Wordsworth, or Browning, or Masefield, or most modern poets.

> '*It is,*' *said Sam,* '*a low-down dirty trick,*
> *To spoil a fellow's work in such a way,*
> *And if you catch him, Dauber, punch him sick,*
> *For he deserves it, be he who he may.*'

> *A seaman shook his old head wise and grey.*
> *'It seems to me,' he said, 'who ain't no judge,*
> *Them drawings look much better now they're smudge.'*

That is Masefield. There is certain realism about it, emphasized by a half-slang phrase or two – 'low-down dirty trick', 'punch him sick' – and the minor grammatical solecism 'them drawings'. It seems far enough away from the direct speech in the frankly romantic poets:

> *Then spoke King Arthur, breathing heavily:*
> *'What is it thou hast seen? or what hast heard?'*
> *And answer made the bold Sir Bedivere*
> *'I heard the water lapping on the crag,*
> *And the long ripple washing through the reeds',*

where Tennyson for his own purposes decks out Malory's simple, almost casual, sentence 'I heard the waters wappe and the waves wanne' with measured and artificial onomatopoeia. Yet there is a difference of kind rather than of degree. In both Masefield and Tennyson speech of the characters has to chime, in metre and general style, with the narrative into which they are introduced. And that is always true. In traditional poetry the language of the speaker cannot escape the demands of rhythm and usually of rhyme; it is inevitably wrested a little – perhaps almost imperceptibly – out of its real colloquial pattern. But so also is the direct speech introduced into the altogether looser metrical forms of today. Unless we admit that the poet, even when he is pretending to report familiar conversation, adds an indefinable something in the very act of acclimatizing the colloquial to his poem as an imaginative whole, we are forced to the conclusion that common speech has of itself some magic poetic quality of its own. Indeed, from this very conclusion arises a fairly widespread heresy in modern criticism, that what is loosely called realism in language can somehow be equated with poetry.

That brings us at once to the subject, and the problem, of verse in the drama. And, since Shakespeare is the most

familiar as well as the greatest English dramatist who uses
this convention, we turn to him for illustration. When we
read Macbeth's outcry on hearing the news of his wife's
death, or, better still, hear it spoken from the stage, we are
conscious of two contradictory things – that in real life he
would never have spoken like that, and that nevertheless,
in the setting of the tragedy, it is precisely how we should
expect him to speak:

> Tomorrow, and tomorrow, and tomorrow,
> Creeps in this petty pace from day to day,
> To the last syllable of recorded time;
> And all our yesterdays have lighted fools
> The way to dusty death. Out, out, brief candle!
> Life's but a walking shadow, a poor player
> That struts and frets his hour upon the stage,
> And then is heard no more; it is a tale
> Told by an idiot, full of sound and fury,
> Signifying nothing.

He is saying, to reduce it to modern colloquial language,
'Life is nothing but a cheat, just one damned thing after
another'. But we feel that our own or any corresponding
Elizabethan expression (whatever that might be) would not
be fitting to that high and dramatic moment. We are content, more than content, to let Macbeth speak with the voice
of Shakespeare.

It is arguable that some, at least, of the poetic phrases in
the plays existed in the ordinary Elizabethan speech of noblemen and the upper classes generally. This idea is amusingly
developed by Bernard Shaw in *The Dark Lady of the Sonnets*:

THE BEEFEATER: I shall not return too suddenly unless
my sergeant comes prowling round. 'Tis a fell sergeant,
sir: strict in his arrest.   Good e'en, sir; and good luck!
He goes.

THE MAN, I.E. SHAKESPEARE: 'Strict in his arrest'! 'Fell
sergeant'![1] [*As if tasting a ripe plum*] O-o-o-h! [*He makes
a note of them*].

[1] *Hamlet* v, ii, 350–1.

But Shakespeare himself (equally playful, perhaps) provides his own evidence of this kind of traffic in speech:

> VIOLA: Most excellent accomplished lady, the heavens rain odours on you!
>
> SIR ANDREW: That youth's a rare courtier. 'Rain odours'! Well!
>
> VIOLA: My matter hath no voice, lady, but to your own most pregnant and vouchsafed ear.
>
> SIR ANDREW: 'Odours', 'pregnant', and 'vouchsafed'. I'll get 'em all three all ready.

This is, however, no more than to say that there was a poetic gusto about Elizabethan speech which is lacking in our own. In that age the common language had a vital, imaginative quality, which tended to be weakened and lost – especially in writing – when, a little later, the age of prose set in.

Yet when we have allowed for this, the fact remains that speech arranged in blank or rhymed verse lines is not natural speech, however much (as in Shakespeare's later plays) the rhythm is broken and disguised. Nevertheless, wherever by its very form and the poetry which is its inspiration it belongs to and heightens the drama, we accept it as natural. On this Mr T. S. Eliot has something to say: 'Whether we use prose or verse on the stage, they are both but means to an end. The difference, from one point of view, is not so great as we may think. In those prose plays which survive . . . the prose in which the characters speak is as remote, for the best part, from the vocabulary, syntax and rhythm of our everyday speech . . . as verse is.'[1] This observation, as far as it relates to prose, is discussed later in the chapter. As far as it relates to verse, or requires the modification which has, in fact, already been hinted at – the verse must occur in the right place, at the right moment. We are back at a canon of literature which has already been, and will be again, emphasized in this book, that form, expression, and theme should be all of a piece; that the play, or any act in it, should be at unity in itself.

[1] *Poetry and Drama* (Theodore Spencer Memorial Lecture, 1950).

This, however, is something of an over-simplification. It equates too easily verse with poetry and prose with the prosaic, and makes a sharp distinction where there is, in reality, a gentle and gradual shading of one into another. The early Elizabethan dramatists commonly wrote their dialogue in rhymed couplets. It was Marlowe who turned 'from jigging veins of rhyming mother-wits' to the 'high astounding terms' of unrhymed verse; and it was Shakespeare himself who, as he grew in experience and stature as a dramatist, by the devices of enjambement, the subtle variation of the caesura, and the weak ending, adapted the blank verse line to speech. In other words, it was early recognized that in a play the verse must conform to what we now call speech rhythm, without the artifice of rhyme. Mr Eliot, in an analysis of the first twenty-two lines of *Hamlet*, shows how Shakespeare, having already 'developed conversational, colloquial verse in the monologue', went further and carried it 'unobtrusively into the dialogue of brief replies':

HORATIO: Friends to this ground.
MARCELLUS: And liegeman to the Dane.
FRANCISCO: Give you good-night.
MARCELLUS: O! farewell, honest soldier. Who hath relieved you?
FRANCISCO: Bernardo has my place.

The argument is briefly, that verse properly used, and not entirely for 'poetic' effect, has the flexibility which makes it a fit instrument for colloquial conversation. In our own time Mr Eliot has sought to illustrate this in his own plays, not indeed by imitating the mature Shakespearian blank verse, but by following, especially in *Murder in the Cathedral*, the earlier model of the mediæval *Everyman*; and more recently Mr Christopher Fry, in, for example, *The Lady's Not For Burning*, has used loosely rhythmical unrhymed lines couched in highly colloquial idiom with such dramatic effect as renders his plays actable and living on the stage.

ALIZON: I'll tell you a strange thing. Humphrey Devize
   Came to the convent to see me, bringing a
    present
   For his almost immediate wife, he said, which
    is me,
   Of barley-sugar and a cross of seed-pearls.
    Next day
   Nicholas came, with a little cold pie, to say
   He had a message from Humphrey. And then
    he sat
   And stared and said nothing until he got up
    to go.
   I asked him for the message, but by then
   It had gone out of his head. Quite gone, you
    see.
   It was curious. – Now you're not speaking
    either.

Even so, it has to be admitted that the passage just quoted,
however dramatically apt, is neither good verse nor good
prose; it has the outward appearance of the one, but little
of the real rhythmical and syntactical texture of the other.
The modern verse dramatist hovers uneasily between two
affectations, prosaic verse and poetic prose. In the older
writers the use of prose and verse was less conscious, and
correspondingly more daring. They often broke down the
regular rhythm of their verse for dramatic purposes; but
they did not make doctrinaire experiments in a mongrel
form. Accordingly, they allowed the language in verse, to
soar into poetry, undisguised and unashamed. True, that
often had the effect of subordinating the drama to the poetry
itself, as Mr Eliot half admits in his comments on the speech
of Marcellus in the passage from *Hamlet* already referred to:

> '*But, look, the morn, in russet mantle clad,*
> *Walks o'er the dew of yon high eastern hill.*'

But there were rich compensations; and the drama survived
– was, in fact, heightened by that very poetic element which

threatened to undo it. When the poetic element really domi-
nates, as in the verse drama of the nineteenth century, like
Stephen Phillips's *Paolo and Francesca*, or in (to take more
august examples) Milton's *Samson Agonistes* and Hardy's
The Dynasts, the work becomes a dramatic poem rather
than a play.

We arrive at the conclusion that verse is properly and
successfully used in the drama only when it has in form,
rhythm, and idiom something of the qualities of prose;
in proportion as it becomes obviously and distinctively
verse it fails. It is allowable because of a basic convention of
the theatre, that everything (including the acting itself) is
larger than life. And this convention, as Mr Eliot says,
applies equally to prose dialogue. We know that in Shakespeare there is a time for prose and a time for verse, though
owing to other conventions they are not always clearly
defined; but the prose of his 'rude mechanicals' and clowns
is heightened for the drama's sake as much as the verse of
his noblemen and kings. Verse and prose are also adjusted
to the occasion. To Falstaff and the rest in the Boar's Head
Tavern Prince Henry talks in prose, but he addresses the
King his father in measured verse:

> *And God forgive them, that so much have sway'd*
> *Your majesty's good thoughts away from me!*
> *I will redeem all this on Percy's head,*
> *And in the closing of some glorious day*
> *Be bold to tell you that I am your son . . .*

There are also differences, clearly observable, in the prose
itself – two in particular: for the courtiers and jesters the re-
partee, the allusive wit, the word-play of a sophisticated and
highly elaborated language, for the lowly people the turns of
expression that belong to ordinary speech; and within each
type there are recognizable modifications, the idiom of dialect, for example, as in the talk of Fluellen, Macmorris, and
Jamy, or of Sir Hugh Evans and Dr Caius in *The Merry
Wives of Windsor*. But we know that the prose speech of, say,
Benedick and Beatrice, or Portia and Jessica, or Rosalind

and Orlando, though (as we assume) it derives from an authentic original, has been touched up by Shakespeare, as has the speech of Bottom, or Dogberry, or the Porter at the gate. There are overtones that belong to the dramatist himself. With him, and to some extent with the other playwrights of the period, fitness in the use of prose and verse, though not always fully achieved, is all. Pistol, whom we might expect to stick to prose, like his associates, nearly always speaks in verse, because he is a stock ranter, but Hamlet and Horatio, who usually (as befits their rank) speak in verse, echo in their courtly accents the earthy prose of the gravediggers when they are standing at the grave of Ophelia. 'Alas! poor Yorick' – when we read that, or Shylock's outburst 'Hath not a Jew hands?', or Bottom's soliloquy on awaking from his dream (that beautiful nonsense), we realize that in this heightening process, this miracle of transmutation worked by the dramatist, not only does the distinction between prose form and verse cease to be relevant, but also prose and poetry meet together.

A play, then, may be written in prose, in verse, or in a mixture of the two. Between the two media there is not an essential difference, but only a difference of degree. The prose play, though it seems nearer to life, since we do, after all, normally converse in prose, follows the same convention of being, in its expression – as, indeed, in everything else – larger than life. 'A speech by a character of Congreve or of Shaw,' says Mr Eliot, 'has – however clearly the characters may be differentiated – that unmistakable personal rhythm which is the mark of a prose style, and of which only the most accomplished conversationalists – who are for that matter usually monologuists – show any trace in their talk.' When we read or hear such a snatch of dialogue as this:

MIRABELL: Here she comes i' faith full sail, with her fan spread and streamers out, and a shoal of fools for tenders.

MRS FAINALL: I see but one poor empty sculler; and he tows her woman after him.

MIRABELL: You seem to be unattended, madam – you

used to have the *Beau-monde* throng after you; and a
flock of gay fine perukes hovering round you.

WITWOOD: Like moths about a candle – I had like to
have lost my comparison for want of breath.

we have a general feeling that this is the kind of conversation
which might take place in the eighteenth century between
such people as Congreve is depicting. But we know that the
elegance, the figures and the 'comparisons' are Congreve's.
So, too, when we hear Joan speaking:

> Well, my loneliness shall be my strength too: it is better
> to be alone with God: His friendship will not fail me, nor
> His counsel, nor His love. In His strength I will dare, and
> dare, and dare, until I die. I will go out now to the common
> people, and let the love in their eyes comfort me for the
> hate in yours. You will all be glad to see me burnt; but
> if I go through the fire I shall go through it to their
> hearts for ever and ever.

We have a sense of the appropriateness of the prose at that
moving moment in the play, but cannot, and do not desire to,
forget that it is Shaw speaking for her, in a language not
merely translated from hers, but utterly refashioned as his
own. The passages quoted are admittedly famous and
memorable; but the general principle underlies all good dramatic prose. In this, as in all other things, the dramatist
works by illusion; in representing the conversation of his
characters he takes advantage of the 'licence of ink'. Indeed,
he can do no other; and he succeeds in proportion as he per-
suades us that from his characters as he conceived them, and
in the play as he has created it, the dialogue is real, credible,
and in the wider sense dramatic.

Before we pass on to the novel, we must consider briefly
the dialogue which is either the vehicle of philosophical
argument or an artifice for developing and sustaining narrative. Of this, in the realm of argument, the Platonic dialogue
is, of course, the classical example – the convention by
which the writer expresses his own theories of life and the

human situation by means of the cut-and-thrust conversation, question and answer, of certain real or imagined characters. Here there is no question of the heightened speech of the drama, but of a literary style cast in dialogue form, in which the writer transfers, as it were, the technique of the stage to the written word. It is the prose equivalent of the dramatic poem. G. R. Malloch's minor (and neglected) classic *The New Republic*, in which a number of recognizable Victorian characters, met together at a house-party, converse on art, literature, and kindred topics, is a direct imitation, a kind of pastiche, of Plato; and we have already seen (p. 57) how Peacock used the same convention in his satirical romances. In these, however, the literary idiom is adapted to the half-personified characters. Peacock's Mr Skionar, the transcendental poet,[1] speaks, for example, in this manner:

> MR SKIONAR: That is a very unpoetical, if not unphilosophical, mode of viewing antiquities. Your philosophy is too literal for our imperfect vision. We cannot look directly into the nature of things; we can only catch glimpses of the mighty shadow in the camera obscura of transcendental intelligence. These six and eighteen are only words to which we give conventional meanings. We can reason, but we cannot feel, by help of them. The tree and the eagle, contemplated in the ideality of space and time, become subjective realities, that rise up as landmarks in the mystery of the past.

Throughout, the spoken prose has an element of exaggeration about it, akin to parody. It is an extension of the symbolism; a modification of the writer's own style appropriated to the types he is depicting. Some of the principles that underlie the use of language in the ordinary drama are transferred, by a natural process, to the printed page.

The greatest example in English of the literary dialogue is Landor's *Imaginary Conversations*, in which classical, historical, literary, and fictional characters are brought to-

[1] *i.e.* Coleridge, in *Crotchet Castle*.

gether and talk on a theme befitting their ghostly encounter. But here the writer takes charge. There are variations in the texture of his prose, but they are related to the matter rather than to any clear and obvious differentiation of characters. The prose is all the time Landor's own, with its peculiar classical chastity united with a limpid English syntax. This could be illustrated from almost any page in the book; but nowhere better than from that conversation between Aesop and Rhodope which has already been twice referred to:

RHODOPE: But, Aesop, you should never say the thing that is untrue.

AESOP: We say and do and look no other all our lives.

RHODOPE: Do we never know better?

AESOP: Yes; when we cease to please, and to wish it; when death is settling the features, and the cerements are ready to render them unchangeable.

RHODOPE: Alas! Alas!

AESOP: Breathe, Rhodope! breathe again those painless sighs: they belong to thy vernal season. May thy summer of life be calm, thy autumn calmer, and thy winter never come!

RHODOPE: I must die then earlier.

AESOP: Laodameia died; Helen died; Leda, the beloved of Jupiter, went before. It is better to repose in the earth betimes than to sit up late; better, than to cling pertinaciously to what we feel crumbling under us, and to protract an inevitable fall. We may enjoy the present, while we are insensible of infirmity and decay; but the present, like a note in music, is nothing but as it appertains to what is past and what is to come. There are no fields of amaranth on this side of the grave; there are no voices, O Rhodope, that are not soon mute, however tuneful; there is no name, with whatever emphasis of passionate love repeated, of which the echo is not faint at last.

There Landor is treating of an eternal theme, the inevitability of change, and the certain onset of death. The effectiveness of this and many other passages derives, of course, from the general conception, 'imaginary conversations'. He might equally have written, say, in indirect speech, or embodied his personal thoughts in an essay. But the technique of direct speech, the device of allowing his characters to speak for him in speaking to one another, gives a special poignancy and force to the things he has to say. Stripped bare of any narrative mechanism the prose has a singleness and unity of its own.

We see this again, though somewhat differently, in two other books where the method of conversation is adopted – Bunyan's *Life and Death of Mr Badman* and Izaak Walton's *The Compleat Angler*. Bunyan's aim is twofold, to tell a story (or, more precisely, to present an imaginary biography) and to moralize upon it. But instead of writing a straightforward narrative with a digressive commentary, as in *The Pilgrim's Progress*, he recounts the iniquitous career of this 'master sinner from a child', and adds his own moral or hortatory observations, through the mouth of Mr Wiseman and Mr Attentive:

ATTEN: Well, Sir, now I have heard enough of Mr Badman's naughtiness, pray now proceed to his Death.

WISE: Why, Sir, the Sun is not so low, we have yet three hours to night.

ATTEN: Nay; I am not in any great hast, but I thought you had even now done with his Life.

WISE: Done! no, I have yet much more to say.

ATTEN: Then he has much more wickedness than I thought he had.

WISE: That may be. But let us proceed: This Mr Badman, added to all his wickedness this, He was a very proud man, a very proud man. He was exceeding proud and haughty in mind; He looked, that what he said, ought not, must not be contradicted or opposed. He counted himself as wise as the wisest in the Countrey, as good as the best, and as beautiful as he that had most of it. But for those that were of an inferior ranck, he would look over them in great contempt. And if at any time he had any remote occasion of having to do with them, he would shew great height, and a very domineering spirit. So that in this it may be said that Solomon gave a characteristical note of him, when he said: Proud and haughty scorner is his name, who dealeth in proud wrath. He never thought his Dyet well enough dressed, his Cloathes fine enough made, or his Praise enough refined.

Again, it is the prose, the very accent of Bunyan himself; but the reader has, if not fully, at least in some measure, the illusion that he is eavesdropping upon a conversation between two of Badman's neighbours not long after the bell had tolled the old reprobate to his grave. In brief – though it must be admitted that Bunyan the preacher far too often breaks in with his homiletics – the dialogue form does not fail of its effect.

Nor does it in Walton, to whom, perhaps, Bunyan owes something:

PISCATOR: Come, hostess, how do you? Will you first give us a cup of your best drink, and then dress this Chub, as you dressed my last, when I and my friend were here about eight or ten days ago? But you must do me one courtesy, it must be done instantly.

HOSTESS: I will do it, Mr Piscator, and with all the speed I can.

PISCATOR: Now, Sir, has not my hostess made haste? and does not the fish look lovely?

VENATOR: Both, upon my word, Sir; and therefore let's say grace and fall to eating of it.

PISCATOR: Well, Sir, how do you like it?

VENATOR: Trust me, 'tis as good meat as I ever tasted. Now let me thank you for it, drink to you and beg a courtesy of you; but it must not be denied me.

PISCATOR: What is it, I pray, Sir? You are so modest, that methinks I may promise to grant it before it is asked.

VENATOR: Why, Sir, it is, that from henceforth you would allow me to call you Master, and that really I may be your scholar; for you are such a companion, and have so quickly caught and so excellently cooked this fish, as makes me ambitious to be your scholar.

The reader, too, is the more ambitious to be Walton's scholar because Piscator's agreeable technicalities and his limpid descriptions of weather, wind, and water are addressed not directly to him but to Venator, Coridon, and the rest, who answer 'by the method' – which is, ultimately, the method of Walton's own simple and evocative prose.

One of the first great works of literary criticism, Dryden's *Essay of Dramatic Poesy*, is cast in the form of a conversation, though not in the strictest dialogue manner:

> Among the rest, it was the fortune of Eugenius, Crites, Lisideus, and Neander, to be in company together; three of them persons whom their wit and quality have made known to all the town; and whom I have chose to hide under these borrowed names, that they may not suffer from so ill a relation as I am going to make of their discourse.

So he introduces his essay. In fact, the four friends talk in miniature essays, with question and comment certainly, but without the cut-and-thrust of true conversation. We are, therefore, always conscious of Dryden himself, though the distribution of the talk among them, on authors and the state of the drama in general, brings a certain freshness and relief. It is significant that the dialogue form encouraged in Dryden a conversational idiom that was to become an important element in the development of English prose style.

We come, then, to the novel; and since the novel is a translation of the drama from the stage to the book, from the spectator and listener to the reader, the dramatist and the novelist observe certain common principles in the recording of the conversation of their characters. True, the correspondence is not exact, because in the play it is attuned to the ear, and in the novel it is conveyed to the reader through the medium of the eye. But the novelist, like the dramatist, has to create the illusion of truth. Having imagined his characters, and placed them in certain situations of his own devising, he has to make them speak in a way that reflects their own individuality. This is especially evident in the 'flat' characters[1] or types, whose idiosyncrasies of speech are usually badges by which we immediately recognize them. 'Under the impression that your peregrinations in this metropolis have not as yet been extensive, and that you might have some difficulty in penetrating the arcana of the Modern Babylon in the direction of the City Road – in short, that you might lose yourself – I shall be happy to call this evening, and instal you in the knowledge of the nearest way.' These are almost the first words of Mr Micawber;[1] and throughout the book, whenever we come upon those rounded periods, we know that it is Mr Micawber speaking. In the same way we know Mr Mantalini, and Mrs Nickleby, and hosts of other Dickens' characters. The trick of speech, the favourite reiterated phrase, the peculiar turn of expression – by this means the novelist keeps such characters living, even though they do not 'live' and develop in the unfolding of the plot.

Not that their conversation always depends on mere tricks; sometimes it is in a general way typical. We have an example of this in the talk of Hardy's flat characters, the yokels and countrymen who form a kind of chorus in the Wessex Novels. Each of these has some recognizable individuality of expression; but they all speak in what is basically the same earthy language, with gleams of poetry in it, a language which we accept rather than recognize as true to life:

'Let en alone,' interposed Joseph Poorgrass. 'The boy's maning is that the sky and the earth in the kingdom of Bath is not altogether different from ours here. 'Tis for our good to gain knowledge of strange cities, and as such the boy's words should be suffered, so to speak it.'

[1] Perhaps it is not quite fair to call Mr Micawber a 'flat' character; but the illustration will serve.

'And the people of Bath,' continued Cain, 'never need to light their fires except as a luxury, for the water springs up out of the earth ready boiled for use'.

' 'Tis true as the light,' testified Matthew Moon. 'I've heard other navigators say the same thing'.

'They drink nothing else there,' said Cain, 'and seem to enjoy it, to see how they swaller it down'.

'Well, it seems a barbarian practice enough to us, but I daresay the natives think nothing o' it,' said Matthew.

It is a kind of speech appropriated to the characters, but overlaid by the imagination of the novelist himself.

'The novelist himself' – we cannot, of course, keep him out of it. In the novel, as in the play, we are a little removed from actuality. 'But,' says Mr James Sutherland,[1] 'in reading a novel we generally know when we are being fobbed off with a piece of literary dialogue'; we know, that is, when the novelist has usurped the part of the very characters he has created. 'When,' goes on Mr Sutherland, 'Mr Rochester tells Jane Eyre that it is just like her to "steal into the vicinage of [her] home along with twilight", or when one of the Rivers girls in the same novel says of Jane, "When in good health and animated, I can fancy her physiognomy would be agreeable", we are not perhaps entitled to say that nobody would ever speak like that – if only because some people do speak like books – but we can say that it has a disconcertingly literary flavour.' Novelists who stray in their creation of character beyond their experience sometimes fall into this error of usurpation – Dickens, for example, in the speech of the upper classes, and Hardy when he moves from the people of the countryside to the intellectuals or a group of noble dames. All this means that true conversation in the novel, though it may not be actual, is appropriate. It sustains the illusion of reality. The novelist has written it up a little, not in quite the same way as the dramatist, but in a way that appeals to the reader rather than to the listener. He has, as it were, overheard, at home, in

[1] Preface to the *Oxford Book of Talk*.

social companionship, in the market-place, the kind of talk he records. It is not real in the detail of phrase and expression; but it is convincing.

We can see this clearly if we think of the novel in terms of time and the background of the story. The idiom of the speech (provided the author has not interfered) is characteristic of the period and the situation or situations represented in the plot. Thus the conversation as well as the narrative of *Tom Jones* has the flavour of the adventurous eighteenth-century road. When we hear (in imagination) Mr Bennet speak, or Elizabeth Bennet, or Mr Darcy, or Elinor Dashwood, we are conscious of that upper-middle-class society in which Jane Austen herself lived and moved, and to which she confined herself in her writing. Or to come a little nearer home, and to take less august examples. If we read in succession Jerome's *Three Men in a Boat* (a very minor classic), a Sherlock Holmes story, an early Wells story, an Aldous Huxley novel, and a modern novel by, say, Graham Greene or Henry Green, we get a fair idea of the changing conversational idiom over the comparatively short period of a little more than half a century. The change is not immediately obvious, but it is there. It follows the progress of events, and naturally moves with the onward march of the language, especially in vocabulary and new colloquialisms, many of them borrowed or derived from American. Indeed, it is not fanciful to see some kind of parallel with the development of transport over the same period, from the bicycle to the motor car and so on to the aeroplane. The speech of today, for example, in actual fact and as it is represented in the novel, has a certain urgency, an impatience of syntactical form, a sharpness and tenseness of vocabulary and expression, that symbolize the age of the jet and atomic power.

Observing, then, certain literary conventions which we all accept, the novelist makes his characters speak, as we say, in character; or, when he does not, forfeits something of our belief in them. He does, or attempts to do, this, not only when he gives his story a contemporary setting, but also when he moves it into a period other than his own – that is,

when he writes a historical novel. But here truth and actuality are only approximations. A novelist lacks first-hand
knowledge of the speech of the past; at best, he can only get
near to it by the study of books and records. It is enough if
he gives us something which suggests the period, as Scott
does, partly by the revival of archaic words and colloquial
expressions. When he fails to do this, we are immediately
aware of it. Thus we realize that the conversation in *West-
ward Ho!* is basically Victorian, touched up a little with a
few Elizabethan tricks. But more commonly the necessity
for a credible period conversational idiom impels the
novelist to adjust his narrative style to it. Of such adjustment the outstanding example is Thackeray's *Henry Esmond*,
where the characters speak as we imagine eighteenth-
century people spoke, and the narrative is written in a
beautiful *pastiche* of eighteenth-century prose. In some other
historical novels – *The Cloister and the Hearth*, for example,
and *Lorna Doone* – the narrative is less directly, yet still
recognizably, adapted to the conversational style. The novelists have deliberately narrowed the gap between their own
normal language and that which they put into the mouth of
characters who are represented as living in another historical
age.

A word must be said here about dialect. Not that any new
principle is involved, for dialect, like any other manner of
speech, is authentic and therefore effective only as it is appropriate to the characters speaking. Mr Sutherland after some
hesitation 'came to the conclusion that dialects were outside
the scope' of the *Oxford Book of Talk*. But we are bound to
accept it in fiction. In actual practice the only one commonly recognized that is separate from standard English, a
kind of language on its own, is the Scotch; and that is most
familiar to us in the Waverley Novels, where Scott uses it
convincingly and to great, sometimes beautiful, effect in the
mouth of his lowlier characters:

    'Ride your ways,' said the gipsy, 'ride your ways, Laird
of Ellangowan – ride your ways, Godfrey Bertram! –

This day have ye quenched seven smoking hearths – see if the fire in your ain parlour burn the blither for that. Ye have riven the thack off seven cottar houses – look if your ain roof-tree stand the faster. – Ye may stable your stirks in the shealings at Derncleugh – see that the hare does not crouch on the hearthstane at Ellangowan. – Ride your ways, Godfrey Bertram – what do ye glower after our folk for? – There's thirty hearts there, that wad hae wanted bread ere ye had wanted sunkets, and spent their life-blood ere ye had scratched your finger. Yes – there's thirty yonder, from the auld wife of an hundred to the babe that was born last week, that ye have turned out o' their bits o' bields, to sleep with the tod and the blackcock in the muirs!'

But for the most part dialects, or local variations of speech, are merely hinted at by the novelists – an odd word here, and a turn of expression there. There are snatches of Mid-landese in the novels of George Eliot and D. H. Lawrence, and wherever an Irishman or a Welshman crops up in a story, his speech has some of the idiosyncrasies of the real thing, as a kind of badge or token. Hardy contents himself with certain eccentricities of pronunciation – '*ithout* for *without*, '*a* for *he*, and the like – and irregular verb forms, like *knowed* and *seed*; unless we assume that some of the poetical turns of expression used by his yokels have their roots in dialect. The representation of class speech – rather than dialect proper – through pronunciation and grammar is most common when the novelist has dealings with what are somewhat loosely called Cockney characters. Of these Sam Weller is an outstanding example:

'Oh, that's it, is it?' said Sam. 'I was afeerd, from his manner, that he might ha' forgotten to take pepper vith that 'ere last cowcumber he eat. Set down, sir; ve make no extra charge for the settin' down, as the king remarked when he blowed up his ministers.'

In brief, the use of dialect or local and class variations of speech is always directed, naturally and legitimately, to the achievement of realistic effect. And the same is true of slang, which, when it passes beyond the confines of colloquialisms that are absorbed into standard speech, is in itself a kind of dialect. There is a slang of Fagin's den as there is a slang of the Drones Club; and both are potent in the portrayal of character, and in the creation of the atmosphere appropriate to the background.

It is, indeed, important to remember, when we read literature, that upon the marches of the literary language stands arrayed this other language of slang. Between the two there is (to shift the metaphor a little) a continual, if not brisk, traffic. Slang is at one remove from colloquial speech; 'language', says the *Shorter Oxford English Dictionary*, 'of a highly colloquial type, considered as below the level of standard educated speech, and consisting either of new words or of current words employed in some special sense'. To turn the pages of Mr Eric Partridge's *Dictionary of Slang*, the standard modern work on the subject, is to be introduced to or reminded of a peculiarly living speech that, though it does not often directly enter the written language (except as an element in the conversation of the play and the novel), has the effect of keeping it, as it were from afar off, fresh and alive. This effect has been heightened in recent years by the impact of American upon English, and the introduction of a great number of American slang terms and phrases into our vocabulary. An hour with *The American Thesaurus of Slang* (Berrey and van den Bark) will reveal what riches there are here. To take an example at random, for the literary phrase 'be humiliated' the following slang synonyms (among others) are given: he laid an egg, come down out of one's pink balloon, come out from under the high hat, come out of the ether, curl up, land with a thud, lay off the lofty lid, let one's hair dry, take off one's high hat, tuck one's tail. In this volume there are 940 sections, each of which has several sub-divisions like, but often much longer than, the one quoted. Many of the words and phrases are, of course, mainly or exclusively American; but many have found their way into English speech, and are becoming familiar in

American books, or English books, especially novels, that
have been influenced by American idiom. Taken together,
Partridge's *Dictionary* and the American *Thesaurus* present
a fascinating and complete picture of a kind of satellite
language that has a life of its own and at the same time gives
new life to the language from which it is evolved.

But, to keep the astronomical figure, slang is not, like the
moon, a dead satellite, though it undergoes, as does the
literary language, within itself the processes of life and death;
that is, in both English and American the slang of today is
not the slang of yesterday. It may be contrasted with
(though the analogy is not altogether sound) the dead satellite which is made up of jargon – in the bad sense – and
cliché and gobbledygook. Both can have an evil influence
upon the parent language – slang, paradoxically, by a
superabundance of life, jargon and the rest by the sterility
of death. The best English, the language of literature, avoids
both the excesses of the one, and the sterile lifelessness of the
other.

2

Thus far the dramatist and the novelist have travelled
pretty much the same road. They both give us through a
written medium, which itself has an inevitable transforming
effect, the kind of talk we hear from all sorts and conditions
of men. But whereas the dramatist leaves it to the actor and
the producer to interpret his dialogue, providing only hints
and instructions in the form of stage directions, the novelist
has to be actor and producer as well as writer. The conversation of his characters has to be embedded in a narrative
that describes the changing scene or background.[1] More-

---

[1] Not quite always, however. One of the most highly praised of
modern novelists, Miss Ivy Compton-Burnett, uses a technique in which
she dispenses with background narrative almost entirely, and sets down
the stylized conversation of her characters (which reminds some critics
of Congreve) as if it were the dialogue in a play. 'Costume and acces-
sories', says another modern novelist and critic, Miss Elizabeth Bowen,
'play so little part that her [Miss Compton-Burnett's] characters some-

over, he has himself to portray the gestures, mannerisms, and general movements of the speaker. In its simplest form, this means nothing more than the use of such expressions as 'He said', 'He asked', 'He answered', with the conventional mechanism of inverted commas to indicate direct speech:

> 'Come, Darcy,' said he, 'I must have you dance. I hate to see you standing about by yourself in this stupid manner. You had much better dance.'

But he may use all kinds of variations of such simple verbs, as *retorted, observed, remarked, continued*; or, going a little further, suggest the precise tone or manner in which the words are spoken with such verbs as *laughed, cried, ejaculated, sneered, stammered*. Nor are these mere casual trivialities. They are one of the means – the simplest – by which he makes the speech of his characters, and therefore the characters themselves, alive.

Beyond this there is the necessity for indicating movement, the action of the character speaking and his relationship to the setting or to the other characters. And here the actual conversation recorded is closely linked with what may be called in general, the narrative. To take one or two examples at random:

> 'I don't know what possessed me, Joe,' I replied, letting his shirt-sleeve go, and sitting down in the ashes at his feet, hanging my head; 'but I wish you hadn't taught me to call knaves at cards, Jacks; and I wish my boots weren't so thick nor my hands so coarse'.

> 'I suppose it would,' said Bell, answering him without a sign of feeling in her voice. But she took in every word that he spoke, and disputed their truth inwardly with all

---

times give the effect of being physically, as well as psychologically, in the nude, and of not only standing and moving about in but actually sitting in thin air.' That she intends as high praise. 'Miss Compton-Burnett', she goes on, 'has stripped the Victorian novel of everything but it's (*sic*) essentials — which must have been fewer than we thought.' There are some readers, of whom I confess myself to be one, who prefer the novel a little more substantially clothed.

the strength of her heart and mind, and with the very vehemence of her soul. 'As if a woman cannot bear more than a man!' she said to herself, as she walked the length of the room alone, when she had got herself free from the doctor's arm.

'Thank ye, thank ye,' said Henchard in a softened voice, his eyes growing downcast, and his manner that of a man much moved by the strains. 'Don't you blame David,' he went on in low tones, shaking his head without raising his eyes. 'He knew what he was about when he wrote that.'

It is clear from these brief passages that conversation and the narrative description that interprets it are all of a piece. The actual speech, in itself often colourless, is heightened and given a particular effect – of humour, intensity, sadness, tragedy – by the modifying phrases or sentences associated with it. To weave the conversation of his characters into the very texture of his own prose, giving it meaning and significance in relation to his narrative, is obviously an important element in the novelist's art. That is why, when a novel is dramatized and translated to the stage, there is always something missing. The actor by his gestures and movements cannot make up for the words in which the novelist describes them. If he is playing Henchard, he may sit with downcast eyes and speak exactly as Hardy indicates; but the actual phrases – 'in a softened voice', 'in low tones', 'shaking his head without raising his eyes' – are, of course, lost; they belong to the novel, a different medium, and are an integral part of its style.

Not that this device of introduction and what the dramatist would call stage direction is always necessary. When he desires to quicken up his dialogue, and let it speak for itself, the novelist often dispenses with it, writing down the conversation with the very minimum of explanatory words. The reader, having been introduced to the speakers, follows their conversation by the actual lay-out of the print on the page, without any indication (as there is in a play) of the name of the person speaking, except as it happens to occur in the dia-

logue. By way of illustration here are two passages, the first
from George Borrow's *Lavengro*, a book which is a cross
between a biography and a novel, and the second, in quite
another key, from a short story by P. G. Wodehouse, where
Bertie Wooster is trying, vainly, to reprove and even dismiss
Jeeves:

'Life is sweet, brother.'

'Do you think so?'

'Think so! There's night and day, brother, both sweet
things; sun, moon, and stars, brother, all sweet things;
there's likewise a wind on the heath. Life is very sweet,
brother; who would wish to die?'

'I would wish to die —'

'You talk like a Gorgio – which is the same as talking
like a fool. Were you a Romany Chal, you would talk
wiser. Wish to die, indeed! A Romany Chal would wish
to live for ever!'

'In sickness, Jasper?'

'There's the sun and stars, brother.'

'In blindness, Jasper?'

'There's the wind on the heath, brother; if I could only
feel that, I would gladly live for ever.'

'I have just met Mr Little, Jeeves,' I said.

'Indeed, sir?'

'He – er – he told me you have been helping him.'

'I did my best, sir. And I am happy to say that matters
now appear to be proceeding smoothly. Whisky, sir?'

'Thanks. Er – Jeeves.'

'Sir?'

'Oh, nothing . . . Not all the soda, Jeeves.'

'Very good, sir.'

He started to drift out.

'Oh, Jeeves!'

'Sir?'

'I wish . . . that is . . . I think . . . I mean . . . oh,
nothing!'

'Very good, sir. The cigarettes are at your elbow, sir. Dinner will be ready at a quarter to eight precisely, unless you desire to dine out?'

'No. I'll dine in.'

'Yes, sir.'

'Jeeves!'

'Sir?'

'Oh, nothing!' I said.

'Very good, sir,' said Jeeves.

There, and wherever a novelist uses this convention, the conversation itself is all-important. He steps aside, realizing that his interference would only distract the attention of the reader, much as an actor's over-attention to stage 'business' is apt to distract the attention of the audience. It goes without saying that at times the novelist in recording what his characters have to say can use indirect instead of direct speech. This he does for convenience, or variation, or economy of words. One example will suffice, which illustrates how effective an element in style the slipping from indirect to direct can be:

So little was Elizabeth disposed to part from him in good humour, that on his making some inquiry as to the manner in which her time had passed at Hunsford, she mentioned Colonel Fitzwilliam's and Mr Darcy's having both spent three weeks at Rosings, and asked him if he was acquainted with the former.

He looked surprised, displeased, alarmed; but with a moment's recollection and a returning smile, replied, that he had formerly seen him often; and, after observing that he was a very gentlemanlike man, asked her how she had liked him. Her answer was warmly in his favour. With an air of indifference he soon afterwards added –

'How long did you say that he was at Rosings?'

'Nearly three weeks.'

'And you saw him frequently?'

'Yes, almost every day.'

It has been said, of both the novel and the play, that the speech, once written down by the author, is removed a little from actuality. That is in general true, even although he uses all the devices of dialect, class speech, grammatical sole-cisms, broken sentences, detached phrases, and the like, to ensure verisimilitude. But the statement requires some modification, especially when we consider certain modern developments in the novel. Speech, after all, derives from thought, and thought is the swiftest thing on earth; it darts about, hither and thither, in an incredible and often discon-certing manner. If, then, the novelist translates, or attempts to translate, thought directly into writing. his prose must follow its incoherent and tortuous ways. There is a classic example in a very early English novel – Sterne's *Tristram Shandy* – where Tristram is made to relate the story (if such it can be called) not as a coherent narrative but as a series of impressions, episodes, episodes within episodes, sudden digressions, which, expressed in a peculiar disconnected (yet oddly beautiful) prose style, represent, as far as it is possible in writing, the spontaneous utterance of the thoughts that succeed one another in the mind:

On the fifth day of November, 1718, which to the aera fixed on, was as near nine kalendar months as any hus-band could in reason have expected, – was I Tristram Shandy, Gentleman, brought forth into this scurvy and disastrous world of ours. – I wish I had been born in the Moon, or in any of the planets, (except Jupiter or Saturn, because I never could bear cold weather) for it could not well have fared worse with me in any of them (though I will not answer for Venus) than it has in this vile, dirty planet of ours, – which, o' my conscience, with reverence be it spoken, I take to be made up of the shreds and clippings of the rest; – not but the planet is well enough, provided a man could be born in it to a great title or to a great estate; or could any how contrive to be called up to publick charges, and employments of dignity or power; – but that is not my case; – and therefore every man will

speak of the fair as his own market has gone in it; – for
which cause I affirm it over again to be one of the vilest
worlds that ever was made . . .

That brings us to the 'impressionistic' or, as it is often called,
the 'stream-of-consciousness' novel. The term 'stream-of-
consciousness' was first used by William James in his *Principles of Psychology*. 'Consciousness does not,' he wrote,
'appear to itself chopped up in bits . . . It is nothing jointed,
it flows . . . Let us call it the stream of thought, or consciousness, or of subjective life.' A quarter of a century later, Miss
May Sinclair applied it to the technique of Miss Dorothy
Richardson's novel *Pointed Roofs* (1915), in which a single
character, Miriam Henderson, thinks aloud and reveals her
thoughts in a more or less coherent soliloquy. 'It is,' she said,
'Miriam's stream of consciousness going on and on.' But
as Mr J. Isaacs says in *An Assessment of Twentieth-Century
Literature*,[1] the technique of disconnected speech representing the swift dartings of thought existed long before the
twentieth century;[2] we have, indeed, already noted it

[1] Chapter III, to which I am indebted for some of the material in the
next few pages, including the quotation from William James, above.

[2] The new psychological approach, in prose and poetry, is 'guyed' in
an amusing skit published during the late eighteen-seventies:

> Across the moorlands of the Not,
>   We chase the gruesome When,
> And hunt the Itness of the What
>   Through forests of the Then.
> Into the inner consciousness
>   We track the crafty Where,
> We spear the Ergo tough, and beard
>   The Ego in his lair.
> With lassoes of the brain we catch
>   The Isness of the Was,
> And in the copses of the Whence
>   We hear the Think bees buzz.
> We climb the skippery Which bark tree,
>   And pause betimes in gnostic rhymes
>   To woo the Over-soul.

The over-soul, of course, belongs to the transcendental philosophy of
Emerson and others.

(though in different form) in *Tristram Shandy*. It sometimes occurs, rather surprisingly, in Jane Austen. There is an interesting example in *Emma*, where the novelist records the 'incessant flow of Miss Bates, who came in talking, and had not finished her speech under many minutes after being admitted into the circle at the fire:

> Ah! dear Mrs Elton, so obliged to you for the carriage! – excellent time. – Jane and I quite ready. Did not keep the horses a moment. Most comfortable carriage. – Oh! and I am sure our thanks are due to you, Mrs Weston, on that score. Mrs Elton had most kindly sent Jane a note, or we should have been. – But two such offers in one day! – Never were such neighbours. I said to my mother, 'Upon my word, ma'am' – Thank you, my mother is remarkably well. Gone to Mr Woodhouse's. I made her take her shawl – for the evenings are not warm – her large new shawl – Mrs Dixon's wedding present. – So kind of her to think of my mother! Bought at Weymouth, you know – Mr Dixon's choice. There were three others, Jane says, which they hesitated about some time. Colonel Campbell rather preferred an olive. My dear Jane, are you sure you did not wet your feet? – It was but a drop or two, but I am so afraid! – but Mr Frank Churchill was so extremely – and there was a mat to step upon – I shall never forget his extreme politeness.

Scott, too, knows the trick. Ellangowan, awaiting nervously the birth of his child, is talking to Guy Mannering and Dominie Sampson:

> 'I cannot weel sleep,' said the Laird, with the anxious feelings of a father in such a predicament, 'till I hear she's gotten ower with it – and if you, sir, are not very sleepy, and would do me and the Dominie the honour to sit up wi' us, I am sure we shall not detain you very late. Luckie Howatson is very expeditious; – there was ance a lass that was in that way – she did not live far from hereabouts – ye needna shake your head and groan, Dominie – I am

sure the kirk dues were a' weel paid, and what can man do mair? – it was laid till her ere she had a sark ower her head; and the man that she since wadded does not think her a pin the waur for the misfortune. – They live, Mr Mannering, by the shore-side, at Annan, and a mair decent, orderly couple, with six as fine bairns as ye would wish to see plash in a salt-water dub; and little curlie Godfrey – that's the eldest, the come o' will, as I may say – he's on board an excise yacht – I hae a cousin at the board of excise – that's Commissioner Bertram; he got his commissionership in the great contest for the county, that ye must have heard of, for it was appealed to the House of Commons – now I should have voted there for the Laird of Balruddery; but ye see my father was a Jacobite, and *out* with Kenmore, so he never took the oaths; and I ken not weel how it was, but all that I could do and say, they keepit me off the roll, though my agent, that had a vote upon my estate, ranked as a good vote for auld Sir Thomas Kittlecourt. But, to return to what I was saying, Luckie Howatson is very expeditious, for this lass —'

Scott himself speaks of the 'desultory and long-winded narrative of the Laird'; but, in essence, he is using the stream-of-consciousness technique.

We have, too, an obvious example in Dickens's Jingle:

'Ah! fine place,' said the stranger, 'glorious pile – frowning walls – tottering arches – dark nooks – crumbling staircases – old cathedral too – earthy smell – pilgrim's feet worn away the old steps – little Saxon doors – confessionals like money-taker's boxes at theatres – queer customers those monks – Popes, and Lord Treasurers, and all sorts of old fellows, with great red faces, and broken noses, turning up, every day – buff jerkins too – match-locks – Sarcophagus – fine place – old legends too – strange stories: capital.'

But this, we suspect, is not quite real; it is an artifice of expression, a typical piece of Dickens's caricature – the 'jingle' of Jingle. Mr Isaacs suggests that the real thing comes rather from Dickens's women, especially Mrs Nickleby and Mrs Lirriper:

> 'Well, then, my love, I wish you would keep your foolish fancy to yourself, and not wake up *my* foolish fancy to keep it company,' retorted Mrs Nickleby. 'Why didn't you think of all this before – you are so careless – we might have asked Miss La Creevy to keep us company or borrowed a dog, or a thousand things – but it was always the way, and was just the same with your poor dear father. Unless I thought of everything —'

Dickens breaks off, and adds the comment: 'This was Mrs Nickleby's usual commencement of a general lamentation, running through a dozen or so of complicated sentences addressed to nobody in particular, and into which she launched until her breath was exhausted.' The phrase 'through a dozen or so of complicated sentences addressed to nobody in particular' gives a hint of a new syntactical idiom as the medium of expression for Mrs Nickleby's acrobatic mind. Yet neither in Dickens himself, nor in the other writers whom Mr Isaacs mentions – Conrad and Samuel Butler among them – do we have a sense of a syntax contrived for the purpose. There is a coherence in incoherence; the sentences are complicated, but they are still, if we admit some stretching of the term, sentences. That is true also of verse. After all, many of the soliloquies in Shakespeare, especially Hamlet's, resolve themselves into streams of consciousness:

> *And thy commandment all alone shall live*
> *Within the book and volume of my brain,*
> *Unmix'd with baser matter: yes, by heaven!*
> *O most pernicious woman!*
> *O villain, villain, smiling, damned villain:*
> *My tables, – meet it is I set it down,*
> *That one may smile, and smile, and be a villain;*
> *At least I'm sure it may be so in Denmark. –*
> *So, uncle, there you are – Now to my word.*

Hamlet's thoughts dart about; but there is still communication with the reader or hearer, in intelligible and recognizably conventional sentences. Browning, it is true, takes the thing further and foreshadows much in the work of later poets:

> Hobbs hints blue, – straight he turtle eats:
> Nobbs prints blue, – claret crowns his cup;
> Nokes outdares Stokes in azure feats, –
> Both gorge. Who fished the murex up?
> What porridge had John Keats?

But here also it is the sudden, abrupt transition of thought, not the syntax, that teases.

Whatever manifestations of the idiom there may have been in earlier writers, the true stream-of-consciousness technique, as we now understand it, does not appear in the novel until the twentieth century. And here the 'stream' metaphor is significant. A stream flows, but its flow is continually broken, as it were, by the pebbles underneath. In the early 'stream-of-consciousness' novels – Miss Dorothy Richardson's for example – the flow is apparent in the paragraph structure. Inside the paragraph the sentences, though sometimes complete, are for the most part of conventional pattern; but they have the effect of running into one another. So, too, in Virginia Woolf. A girl – Rhoda – is going away for the summer holidays. Her thoughts follow one another, in a kind of sympathy with the moving train:

The train now stamps heavily, breathes stertorously, as it climbs up and up. At last we are on the top of the moor. Only a few wild sheep live here; a few shaggy ponies; yet we are provided with every comfort; with tables to hold our newspapers, with rings to hold our tumblers. We come carrying these appliances with us over the top of the moor. Now we are on the summit. Silence will close behind us. If I look back over that bald head, I can see silence already closing and the shadows of clouds chasing each other over the empty moor; silence closes over our transient passage. This I say is the present moment; this is the first day of the summer holidays. This is part of the emerging monster to whom we are attached.

These two apparently conflicting though really complementary characteristics, brokenness and flow, may also be represented by extremes in syntactical pattern. Here for examples we have to go to the master of this technique, James Joyce, whose two most famous novels, *Ulysses* and *Finnegans Wake*, record respectively the thoughts of a man during a single day and the dreams of a man during a single night. On the one hand, the sentences are truncated, often verbless, reduced sometimes to a single word. Leopold Bloom – the hero (if that is the apt term) of *Ulysses* – is at a funeral, thinking of the widow of the man about to be buried:

He looked down at the boots he had blacked and polished. She had outlived him, lost her husband. More dead for her than for me. One must outlive the other. Wise men say. There are more women than men in the world. Condole with her. Your terrible loss. I hope you'll soon follow him. For Hindu widows only. She would marry another. Him? No. Yet who knows after? Widowhood not the thing since the old queen died. Drawn on a gun-carriage. Victoria and Albert. Frogmore memorial mourning. But in the end she put a few violets in her bonnet. Vain in her heart of hearts. All for a shadow. Consort not even a king. Her son was the substance. Something new to hope for not like the past she wanted back, waiting. It never comes. One must go first: alone, under the ground: and lie no more in her warm bed.

On the other hand, they may slide into one another, unpunctuated, making one continuous flowing whole. Leopold Bloom's wife is engaging in what Mr Isaacs calls a 'gigantic silent monologue' concerning her memories of Spain:

'and the wineshops half open at night and the castanets and the night we missed the boat at Algeciras the watch-

man going about serene with his lamp and O that awful
deepdown torrent O and the sea crimson sometimes like
fire and the glorious sunsets and the figtrees in the Ala-
meda gardens yes and all the queer little streets and pink
and blue and yellow houses and the rosegardens and the
jessamine and geraniums and cactuses and Gibraltar as a
girl where I was a Flower of the mountain yes when I
put the rose in my hair like the Andalusian girls used or
shall I wear a red yes and how he kissed me under the
Loorish wall and I thought well as well him as another
and then I asked him with my eyes to ask again yes and
then he asked me would I yes to say yes my mountain
flower and first I put my arms around him yes and drew
him down to me so he could feel my breasts all perfume
yes and his heart was going like mad and yes I said yes I
will Yes.'

Or, in the extremes of *Finnegans Wake*, words themselves
sometimes cohere or are blurred in queer but often suggestive coagulations:

Soft morning, city! Lsp! I am leafy speafing. Lpf! Folty
and folty all the nights have falled on to long my hair.
Not a sound, falling, Lispn! No wind no word. Only a
leaf, just a leaf and then leaves. The woods are fond
always. As we were their babes in. And robins in crews so.
It is for me goolden wending. Unless? Away! Rise up,
man of the hooths, you have slept so long! Or is it only so
mesleems? On your pondered palm. Reclined from cape
to pede. With pipe on bowl. Terce for a fiddler, sixt for
makmerriers, none for a Cole. Rise up now and aruse!
Norvena's over. I am leafy, your goolden so you called
me, may me life, yea your goolden, silve me solve,
exsogerraider! You did so drool. I was so sharm. But
there's a great poet in you too.

In the conventional manner the same effect, though less
realistic, is produced by indirect recording of the various
objects of thought, which are linked together by the usual

syntactical plus sign (*and*). Here, for example, is Lytton Strachey imaginatively analysing the mind of the dying Queen Victoria:

> Perhaps her fading mind called up once more the shadows of the past to float before it, and retraced, for the last time, the vanished visions of that long history – passing back and back, through the cloud of years, to older and ever older memories – to the spring woods at Osborne, so full of primroses for Lord Beaconsfield – to Lord Palmerston's queer clothes and high demeanour, and Albert's face under the green lamp, and Albert's first stag at Balmoral, and Albert in his blue and silver uniform, and the Baron coming in through a doorway, and Lord M. dreaming at Windsor with the rooks cawing in the elm-trees, and the Archbishop of Canterbury on his knees in the dawn, and the old King's turkey-cock ejaculations, and Uncle Leopold's soft voice at Claremont, and Lehzen with the globes, and her mother's feathers sweeping down towards her, and a great old repeater-watch of her father's in its tortoise-shell case, and a yellow rug, and some friendly flounces of sprigged muslin, and the trees and the grass at Kensington.

It is not hard to see that, for a fictional character, such musings could be easily translated into the 'stream-of-consciousness' idiom. Not, indeed, that the new idiom is to be found in all modern novelists. Far from it. A great many of them stick to the syntactical conventions, though their language is often modelled on, or influenced by, the colloquial realism that is characteristic of American fiction.

3

It has been said by some modern critics that Joyce 'rejuvenated language'. In as far as this means that by making it more flexible both in syntax and vocabulary he bridged the gap between thought itself and its expression in words this is no doubt true. There is in part a return to the freedom and fluidity of Shakespeare and his contemporaries before syntax settled into a more or less fixed and conventional pattern, hedged about by the 'rules' of the grammarians. On the literary significance of the stream-of-consciousness method it is not the intention of this book to pronounce; but certainly it has had a considerable influence on much modern writing in prose and verse. In prose this is most apparent in the novel, and, not unnaturally, most of all in the dialogue. The psychological workings of the mind are not to be expressed in the ordinary subject-predicate syntax of the sentence. Here Mr Eliot's dictum about the speech of prose (p. 86) requires some modification. The idiom is plain, for example, though by no means extreme, in the following short passage from Mr Joyce Cary's *The Horse's Mouth*:

> Sara came in again blowing like an engine, and said, 'Oh dear, I get so short of breath since I had the 'flu. Excuse me leaving you, Miss Coker. The kettle is just on. You'll have some tea, won't you? Yes, of course, I meant to write a long time ago, but the children got away with my pen. You know what they are.'
> 'We came about these pictures, Mrs Monday. Which you sold to Mr Hickson, having no right to them.'
> 'That's right, Miss Coker.'
> 'I don't call it right. I call it a robbery.'
> 'That's right. Won't you sit down, Miss Coker. Why, Gulley, it's a real pleasure. Of course, Mr Hickson said the pictures weren't properly finished and we owed a lot of money all round, and Mr Jimson had gone away and I didn't know when he was coming back, so when Mr Hickson said he'd pay all the debts and give me a bit to carry on, just for some of the pictures lying about, I was in such a whirl I didn't know how to say no.'

There the sentences, though tolerably normal, have the incoherence of a voluble woman – who is, in the story, playing for time – and the two contrasted characteristics of brokenness and flow. Mr Henry Green, who is noted for his naturalistic dialogue, goes a little farther, mainly by the device of a deliberately loose punctuation. The mistress of the house (in *Loving*) is remonstrating with her butler:

> She laughed and faced him. 'Oh yes the shops will be using that as an excuse for everything soon. Mind I'm not blaming anyone,' she said, 'but it's going to be hopeless. Now Raunce I'm so very worried about these nursery meals.'
> 'Yes Madam.'
> She began to smile, as though pleading with him. 'I want your help. Everyone is being so very awkward. Nanny has complained that the food is quite cold by the time it gets to the nursery and Mrs Welch tells me it leaves the kitchen piping hot so what am I to believe?'
> They looked long at each other. At last he smiled.
> 'I'm sure Albert carries the meals up soon as ever they are served,' he said. 'But if it would be of any assistance Madam I'll take them up myself for the next few days.'
> 'Oh thank you Raunce, yes that is good of you. Now I promised Michael I would go along, why was it he wanted me? Yes well that will be all.' She started off to the head gardener. She did not get far. Miss Burch stopped her in the Long Passage.
> 'Could I speak to you for a moment Madam?'
> 'Yes Agatha?'
> Before going on Miss Burch waited until Raunce, who was leaving Mrs Jack's room, should be out of earshot.
> 'It's Kate Madam. I wouldn't bother you Madam only it does seem not right to me that a slip of a girl can take him his tea first thing while he lies in bed there.'
> 'Whose tea good heavens?'
> 'Arthur Madam.'
> 'We must call him Raunce Agatha. It does sound absurd I know. What's more I don't like that name.' Her voice had taken a teasing note. 'I think we shall have to change it don't you?'

To some extent, this conversational idiom has spread to, or influenced, syntactical usage in other departments of the novel – its narrative and description. I have given an example from the early Joyce in *Better English* (p. 171). So, too, in Joyce Cary (*The Horse's Mouth*), though since here the descriptive narrative is autobiographical – that is, in the first person – it may be identified with the actual stream-of-consciousness:

> The sun had crackled into flames at the top; the mist was getting thin in places, you could see crooked lines of grey, like old cracks under spring ice. Tide on the turn. Snake broken up. Emeralds and sapphires. Water like varnish with bits of gold leaf floating thick and heavy. Gold is the metal of intellect. And all at once the sun burned through in a new place, at the side, and shot out a ray that hit the Eagle and Child, next the motor boat factory, right on the new signboard.
>
> A sign, I thought. I'll try my old friend Coker. Must start somewhere. Coker, so I heard, was in trouble. But I was in trouble and people in trouble, they say, are more likely to give help to each other than those who aren't. After all, it's not surprising, for people who help other people in trouble are likely soon to be in trouble themselves. And then, they are generally people too who enjoy the consolation of each other's troubles. Sympathetic people. Who'd rather see each other's tears, boo-hoo, than the smile of a millionaire, painted in butter on a barber's shave.

There are three other interesting and characteristic elements here – the metaphorical imagery of the first paragraph, the deliberate echoing of words (*trouble, people*) in the second, and the symbolic interpolation (*boo-hoo*) after the word *tears*.

Some novelists resort to a manipulation of syntax for the purpose of introducing word effects. In *Better English* I have given some examples from Miss Elizabeth Bowen, which I reproduce here. They are all taken from her novel *The Heat of the Day*:

(i) The use of the inflected (apostrophe *s*) possessive for other than personal pronouns:

'Nothing but the fire's flutter and the clock's ticking'; 'another post's bomb'; 'the lamp's dazzling shade'; 'on the restaurant's wall'; 'the senses' harmony'; 'these hundreds of books' indifference'.

(ii) The use of repetitive stammer, common also in much modern verse:

They need not come coming round after her.
An hour ago, perhaps, what had been being said had become not necessary.
Who was it who was here whom I didn't know?

(iii) The use of exaggerated inversion:

– decapitated, he said he shouldn't wonder if many of them were.

(iv) A deliberate variation in normal word order and phrase grouping. In the last two sentences there is again the repetitive stammer:

The restaurant at which they met most often was this morning, he was sorry to tell her, closed.
She was thinking, was this to be, after all, all?
In the street below, not so much a step as the semi-stumble of someone after long standing shifting his position could be, for the first time by her, heard.

There are similar tricks or idiosyncrasies in the novels of Mr Henry Green, in particular his use of the adjective form where in conventional English we should expect the adverb: 'He said friendly', 'Raunce eyed her very sharp', 'He spoke uneasy', ' "Very good Madam", Burch said grim'.

But this recognition of a fluidity in the parts of speech is a return to, and in certain ways an extension of, an older usage. 'But me no more buts' – in Shakespeare there is a happy freedom of noun, verb, adjective, adverb, and pre-position. The traditional divisions maintained by the grammarians, often to the point of pedantry, have always had a somewhat cramping effect on conventional writing, especially prose. Rather surprisingly, it was Hazlitt who, in his unjustly neglected *Grammar*, enunciated a philosophy of the parts of speech that was at variance with the formal definitional system of contemporary grammarians:

> The parts of speech are the different sorts of words of which a sentence is composed. This difference does not, however, arise from any intrinsical difference in the ideas to which those words relate, or from the nature of the things spoken of, but from our manner of speaking of them. The grammatical distinctions of words are intended to show their use in *construction*, or in reference to other words in the same sentence. Words, considered nakedly in themselves, are the names or signs of certain things; words, as parts of speech, *i.e.* as component parts of a sentence, are the names or signs of certain things, accompanied with an intimation in what manner they are joined together in the mind of the speaker, and made the subjects of discourse.

This argument has been elaborated and developed by modern grammarians, especially Sweet and Jespersen. As a matter of fact, it merely emphasizes the fact, which is implicit even in the traditional classification, that the difference between the parts of speech lies in function, not meaning; but it does allow of a greater flexibility in expression. Even modern pedants have objected, vainly and illogically, to the increasing use of what is usually called the attributive noun and the passing of noun into verb. But a greater freedom in modern usage, to which journalism has largely contributed, has had the effect of giving force and vividness to the language. 'At Hounslow West a 300-yard queue snaked out of the station' – so runs a sentence in the evening paper I have just bought; and a syntactical compression ('300-yard queue', 'snaked') gives it both directness and economy.

There are today extremes in prose, as well as in verse. The reviewer of a modern novel says of it: 'The writing at its best is wonderfully evocative; but occasionally it is strained almost to desperation, so clamped and contorted that it hardly communicates with the reader. Take, for instance, a felicity strained to deformity:

> A miser was I of myself: fearful wrong, so to hide, delight no good heart with me knowing; my clothes and I hid me; all hide me; this life's purpose – hiding myself.' [1]

Now, whatever felicity there is in that is certainly lost in a 'clamped and contorted' syntax – a syntax which in parts is, not to put too fine a point upon it, unintelligible. But extremes apart, there is a kind of dichotomy in modern prose style. In imaginative writing, the novel, there is often a 'bending' of syntax to the matter, to the psychological motions of thought, to such devices as the 'flash-back', which interrupt the time-flow of the story. But the prose which (to use Hazlitt's phrase again) is 'an unvarnished medium to convey ideas' – the prose, that is, of the essay, the journalistic leader, criticism, biography, exposition – still follows the normal syntactical pattern, only modified, if it is modified at all, by occasional American turns of expression. The reviewer of even the most 'advanced' novel himself writes in sentences whose construction is conventional. What the outcome of this present struggle between experiment and tradition will be it is too early yet to say. No doubt traditional syntax is being gradually and imperceptibly modified, as indeed it has been throughout the history of the language. Experiment always belongs to a particular period; it represents, by extremes, a phase of development, and so contributes to development as a whole.

Indeed, the awareness of the ambiguities and overtones in words, sharpened by the modern study of semantics, is having an influence on syntactical construction and idiom, not only in imaginative writing (especially poetry) but also on expository prose. I cannot illustrate this better than by quoting a reviewer [2] of my previous book *Better English*.

---

[1] Edwin Muir in *The Observer*, June 5, 1955.
[2] Mr T. C. Worsley in *The New Statesman*, June 18, 1955

In that book I had criticized a sentence of the reviewer's own, 'Our judgement over them is suspended', suggesting that for *over* he should have written *of*. Syntactically, or idiomatically, the correction is sound; in what may be called for convenience 'standard' English, we can say 'my judgement *of*' or 'We pass judgement *on* or *upon*', but not 'judgement *over*'. But the reviewer passes beyond the realms of syntax: 'My preposition (if a measure of boasting may be permitted) is rich in ambiguities of the Empsonian kind.[1] *Over* brings with it the idea that we are above them – on that eminence from which judicial judgement is given. There is, as well, the faint suggestion that our judgement hangs above them like a Sword of Damocles, and this shade of feeling colours the last word of the sentence, *suspended*, giving it almost the force of a double sense. My sentence, in brief, is meant to carry overtones with it (whether it does or not); the pedant's emendation makes it insipid, flavourless and flat'.

That, as we say in an expressive modern idiom, is fair enough. The reviewer was moving in the exalted realms of feeling, while I (the pedant) was crawling about in what Milton no doubt would have called the cool regions of usage. In effect, this is only an extension of a common syntactical device known as the 'pregnant construction', a construction 'in which more is implied than the words express' (SOED). Fowler (MEU) gives the simple example 'Put it in your pocket', which means 'put it into, and keep it in, your pocket'. But the pregnant construction works within the realm of normal syntax and meaning. Here the reviewer, in endowing his expression with 'pregnancy', has defied syntactical idiom in the word *over*, and charged the word *suspended* with a metaphorical sense that originates in a classical allusion. Whether, in fact, that preposition *over* and the verb *suspended* do suggest to the reader a kind of all-judging Jove and the image of the Sword of Damocles is, I think, open to question. If not, the overtones belong to the writer alone; the communication between writer and reader

[1] See p. 61.

is imperfect. He is using a private language, and a private syntax, of his own; and if the reader, unable to follow him into his privacy, misses something of his meaning, the writer has no real grounds for complaint.

For the simple fact remains – I return to an argument which has cropped up once or twice in these pages – that usage in English is a real thing, not a mere perverse fantasy of the grammarians. In a notice of Mr F. L. Lucas's recent book, *Style*, a reviewer said with a sneer, 'Our master today is still that disarming Samuel Smiles of the 'twenties, H. W. Fowler'. But the sneer is misplaced. Neither Fowler nor Partridge pretends to write for genius; but there is no reason why any writer who falls below the level of genius – in whom inspired imagination is not strong enough to exempt him from the obligations of ordinary men – should fly to a syntax of his own, or cover up poverty of thought with a convenient blanket of meaningless verbiage or syntactical aberrations. The truth is that many writers today of mediocre talent, or no talent at all, cultivate a studied obscurity that only too often deceives the critics, who tend to be afraid that behind a smoke-screen of words they are missing the effectual fire, and so for safety's sake give honour where no honour is due. 'He has the highest aims, and writes metaphysical verses,' says another reviewer, 'in which a locution such as "a seem that cannot is" takes its natural lucid place.' [1] Unless the critic is talking with his tongue in his cheek, he is affecting to find a natural lucidity where the poet himself seems, in the cause of metaphysical ingenuity, to have flung lucidity to the winds.

The highly specialized study of semantics is difficult for the ordinary layman. It is, basically, only a conscious extension of one's normally unconscious acceptance of the idea that words are not absolutes but variables in both function and meaning; that what a speaker speaks or a writer writes may mean one thing to himself, and various things to his various readers. The semanticist always tends to protest too

[1] Mr Rayner Heppenstall in *The New Statesman and Nation* (September 23, 1955).

much. It needs no ghost come back to Denmark – or, indeed, no learned semanticist – to remind us that in the language of modern political propaganda no ultimate fixed meaning can be assigned to such words as 'liberty', 'freedom', 'communist', 'democracy'. True, in the propaganda itself this assumption is made; but the ordinary man, who ten to one has never heard of semantics, is not quite so gullible as the semanticist likes to imagine.

Certainly, in the realm of literature the reader is constantly confronted with the necessity for what may be called semantic interpretation; if, that is, he is to understand and appreciate fully the inward meaning which a writer intends to convey and the effects he wishes to produce. But this necessity he tacitly accepts, even when he is not capable of a complete imaginative interpretation. It does not require abnormal insight on his part to realize that in the sentence

> *For every man hath business and desire,*
> *Such as it is*

the word *business* has an emotive content that it lacks in the expressions 'a grocery business' or 'Business is prospering'; and that in the lines

> *Our vegetable love shall grow*

the word *vegetable* has certain overtones that are not present in it when we speak of 'vegetable marrow' or 'vegetable soup'. After all, the basis of semantics is the familiar principle that in a living language the words themselves are living; no less and no more. It is a science, not a piece of linguistic magic designed to excuse or elucidate some of the more recondite passages in modern literature; nor is it (as some semanticists seem to suggest) a philosophical study that makes nonsense of syntactical grammar. Grammar in its proper relationship to usage has its own sphere; and the true grammarian, like the semanticist himself, is alive to the 'livingness' of the language whose usage he analyses and records.

4

Of oratory, the kind of prose that is fashioned (and often actually written beforehand) for speaking in public, there is only this to be said, that the sentences are designed rhythmically for the ear, and are often, though not always, heightened by a pictorial imagery that appeals to the imagination. This can best be illustrated by three examples, the first from a sermon of John Donne, the second from a speech by Edmund Burke, the third from John Bright's speech on the Crimean War:

The Bell doth toll for him that thinkes it doth; and though it intermit againe, yet from that minute, that that occasion wrought upon him, hee is united to God. Who casts not up his Eie to the Sunne when it rises? but who takes off his Eie from a Comet when that breakes out? Who bends not his eare to any bell, which upon any occasion rings? but who can remove it from that bell, which is passing a peece of himselfe out of this world? No man is an Iland, intire of it selfe; every man is a peece of the Continent, a part of the maine; if a Clod bee washed away by the Sea, Europe is the lesse, as well as if a Promontorie were, as well as if a Mannor of thy friends or of thine owne were; any mans death diminishes me, because I am involved in Mankinde; And therefore never send to know for whom the bell tolls; It tolls for thee.

The last cause of this disobedient spirit in the Colonies is hardly less powerful than the rest, as it is not merely moral, but laid deep in the natural constitution of things. Three thousand miles of ocean lie between you and them. No contrivance can prevent the effect of this distance in weakening Government. Seas roll, and months pass, between the order and the execution; and the want of a speedy explanation of a single point is enough to defeat a whole system. You have, indeed, winged ministers of vengeance, who carry your bolts in their pounces to the remotest verge of the sea. But there a power steps in, that limits the arrogance of raging passions and furious elements, and says, 'So far shalt thou go, and no farther'. Who are you, that should fret and rage, and bite the chains of Nature? Nothing worse happens to you than does to all Nations who have extensive Empire; and it happens in all the forms into which Empire can be thrown.

I do not suppose that your troops are to be beaten in actual conflict with the foe, or that they will be driven into the sea; but I am certain that many homes in England in which there now exists a fond hope that the distant one may return – many such homes may be rendered desolate when the next mail shall arrive. The angel of death has been abroad throughout the land; you may almost hear the beating of his wings. There is no one, as when the first-born were slain of old, to sprinkle with blood the lintel and the two side posts of our doors, that he may spare and pass on; he takes his victims from the castle of the noble, the mansion of the wealthy, and the cottage of the poor and the lowly, and it is on behalf of all these classes that I make this solemn appeal.

Donne's tolling of the bell, and his vivid geographical figure; Burke's picture of the sounding, separating seas; Bright's great analogy of the Passover angel, with its moving Biblical appeal – all these 'came home to men's business and bosoms' in the first place as they listened, and afterwards, for their posterity, in the printed word. The peculiar pictorial effects of that older oratory are no longer in fashion. Public speech during the last century has grown nearer private speech, yet with the difference that the actual sentences are so fashioned, in cumulative and antithetical effect, as to be memorable. Of this the famous speech of Abraham Lincoln at Gettysburg is a notable example:

The world will little note, nor long remember, what we say here, but it can never forget what they did here. It is for us, the living, rather to be dedicated here to the unfinished work they have thus far so nobly advanced. It is rather for us to be here dedicated to the great task remaining before us, that from these honored dead we take increased devotion to that cause for which they here gave the last full measure of devotion; that we here highly resolve that the dead shall not have died in vain, that the nation shall, under God, have a new birth of freedom, and that the government of the people, by the people, and for the people, shall not perish from the earth.

There is throughout a curious echoing effect – 'will little note, nor long remember . . . but it can never forget', 'for us rather to be dedicated here . . . rather for us to be here dedicated', 'we take increased devotion . . . they here gave the last full measure of devotion', 'for us, the living . . . from these honored dead' – and, at the end, a reiterative climax achieved by the repetition of the word *people*, and a cumulative use of prepositions. This significant use of words, the balance of the sentence, and the device of climax is, rather than deliberate pictorial imagery, the chief element in the speech of the greatest modern orator, Sir Winston Churchill:

I would say to the House, as I said to those who have joined this Government: 'I have nothing to offer but blood, toil, tears and sweat'. . . . You ask, what is our aim? I can answer in one word: Victory – victory at all costs, victory in spite of all terror, victory, however long and hard the road may be; for without victory, there is no survival. Let that be realized; no survival for the British Empire; no survival for all that the British Empire has stood for, no survival for the urge and impulse of the ages, that mankind will move forward towards its goal. But I take up my task with buoyancy and hope. I feel sure that our cause will not be suffered to fail among men.

Our own day has seen the development of a new technique of public speech, in wireless broadcasting, where the speaker has to prepare a written script that sounds, when it is read, like the ordinary colloquial spoken word.

As the broadcasters frequently publish their talks, this 'armchair' idiom is often seen in the permanence of print, and therefore represents a particular type of modern prose. Its chief characteristics are a familiar, 'undress' vocabulary and idiom; a comparatively loose syntax, with direct questions, exclamations or polite imperatives, occasional broken sentences – and frequent parentheses; and a plentiful use of personal pronouns. Indeed, since the broadcaster's aim is so to speak his thoughts aloud that they 'get over' to the listener by the fireside, he uses a kind of modified 'stream-of-consciousness' technique. It is significant that in their printed form these talks are usually revised a little – a reminder of an essential, if slight, difference between the spoken and the written word. But the talk as presented to the eye has still the accent of the microphone. Here, by way of example, are two short passages from fairly recent broadcasts, the first, on a literary theme, by the late Professor George Gordon, and the second, on a scientific topic, by Mr Fred Hoyle of St John's College, Cambridge. In both the characteristics outlined above are plain to see; the idiom of speech is uppermost:

The most important thing about Pepys's *Diary* is that we were never meant to see it. There's interest for you! Every reader of Pepys enjoys, that is to say, from start to finish, 'the fearful pleasure of the key-hole' – of seeing and hearing what he was never intended to see or hear. Pepys took great precautions: wrote it in shorthand (with various dodges to make the script more difficult), and wrote it in his office after hours, when all the clerks had gone. He kept it locked up there; for if he had taken it home, his wife, 'poor wretch', as he calls her, might have asked questions. He carried it on for eight and a half years, till his eyes grew weak – from 1660, when he was twenty-seven, to 1669, when he was thirty-six – putting down all his doings, and all his little motives, with perfect honesty. There is hardly an erasure in his script: down it went, and stood there. The result is the frankest and most intimate book in print.

My main purpose tonight is to tell you what the astrophysicists have discovered recently about the inner workings of the Sun. And this will bring up their answers to a number of age-old cosmological questions. What is the Sun made of? How hot is it? Is it simply hot on its surface, or is the whole body hot, inside and outside? These are some of the things which puzzle people. Much more important is this one. What is the source of the Sun's energy? Is it growing hotter or colder? How long will it continue to radiate light and heat at just the rate required by living creatures on the Earth? Is it getting smaller and smaller, or will it stay the same size – or even perhaps get bigger? Some of these questions, I might warn you, will take us forwards into the remote future, perhaps to a time more than 10,000,000,000 years hence.

That kind of writing has, of course, certain merits – even a certain individuality – of its own; it may have an influence on the development of certain forms of prose, especially the critical or expository essay. But it is safe to say that had Professor Gordon and Mr Hoyle been addressing the reader directly, they would have written differently.

CHAPTER VI

RHYTHM IN PROSE AND VERSE

IT HAS been suggested that the 'underlying element in verse is the recurrence of sound', and that this recurrence is represented in such technical qualities or artifices as alliteration, rhythm, rhyme, repetition, and association of sound and sense. Of these qualities rhythm is the most important, because it is a basic principle of the spoken language, whether prose or verse. In the speaking of any sentence, or the enunciation of a polysyllabic word, some syllables are lightly and some are heavily stressed. This is especially true of English, a language in which stress is far more strongly marked than it is, say, in French. Rhythm may be described as the sound pattern made by the rise and fall of the stresses in speech. In prose this pattern is irregular, as a couple of sentences taken at random will illustrate. The unstressed syllables are unmarked, the stressed are marked (/), and those with a medium stress are marked (\\):

Out of this concourse of several hundred people, perhaps half of whom were directly connected with the writing trade, there was not a single one who could point out that freedom of the Press, if it means anything at all, means the freedom to criticize and oppose. Significantly, no speaker quoted from the pamphlet which was ostensibly being commemorated.

Different readers would, of course, read that passage in different ways, and insert their marks of stress accordingly. But they would have a certain measure of agreement; and would certainly agree that the full stresses (/) fall at irregular intervals. It is plain that that is not true of verse, or at any rate of what we commonly think of as verse:

> The cúrfew tólls the knéll of párting dáy,
> The lówing hérd winds slówly o'ér the léa;
> The ploúghman hómeward plóds his wéary wáy
> And leáves the wórld to dárkness ánd to me.

There the stresses seem (if we are prepared to manœuvre and exaggerate a little) to fall regularly, and, because of that, verse arranges itself, or is arranged, in measured lines; it has, in short, a metrical structure.

This outward, technical difference between the two forms of writing, prose and verse, is for the most part easily recognized. We distinguish a piece of verse from a piece of prose when we hear it spoken, or when we see it in print. True, there are times when they are not readily distinguishable, either in quality or technical form. But in general we may say of prose that it has none of the conscious artifices of verse, especially rhyme, and that since in it the stresses do not fall regularly it cannot be measured into lines or 'verses'; to put it another way, having no regular rhythm, prose has no metre.

But, though irregular, the rhythm is there – *rhuthmos*, the 'flow' of the sound, its rise and fall in the unmeasured sentences. And because it is irregular, it cannot be displayed in a kind of diagrammatic picture as can the regular rhythm of verse. For of necessity the rhythm of prose is infinitely variable. True, in his monumental work *A History of English Prose Rhythm* Professor Saintsbury has scanned in detail certain prose passages to point his argument. But it is difficult to see to what purpose. He takes, for example, the prayer of St Chrysostom in the English *Book of Common Prayer*. 'This very remarkable piece,' he says, 'which, I believe, was taken straight from the Greek, not only allows itself to be scanned with unusual confidence, but makes it, in a still more unusual manner, possible to observe some method in the music.' And so, dividing it into hypothetical bars or feet, he depicts its rhythmical pattern like this:

Almighty | God, | who hast given | us grace | at this time |
with one accord | to make | our common | supplications |
unto thee, | and dost promise | that when two | or three |
are gathered | together | in thy Name | thou wilt grant |
their requests: | Fulfil now, | O Lord | the desires | and
petitions | of thy servants | as may be most | expedient |
for them, | granting us | in this world | knowledge | of
thy truth, | and in the world | to come | life everlasting.[1]

It is difficult to see what significance or value there is in such
scansion. Indeed, the division into feet only serves to
obscure the natural (and beautiful) flow of the rhythm. But
there is a significance in Saintsbury's introductory note.
Evidently he considers it an excellent thing that in this
passage a rhythmic pattern is recognizable – 'it allows itself
to be scanned with unusual confidence' – and that it is
possible to 'observe some method in the music'. As a
matter of fact, he exaggerates both the pattern and the
method, though his system of marks and bars does little
to make them plain. Whatever combination of feet there
may be according to Saintsbury's fantastic table given at the
beginning of his book, the fact remains that the rise and fall
of the sound, admittedly pronounced, in this collect has
the irregularity of prose, not that 'recurrence' which we
associate with verse. It is not, therefore, amenable to
analysis based on an artificial system of metrical feet. Any
divisions that indicate or suggest rhythm are phrasal,
representing an alliance of sound, syntax, and meaning. In
this passage, for example, we have after the initial ascription
('Almighty God'), two rising rhythmical waves that finally
break, as it were, in the strong accentuation of 'Fulfil now,
O Lord', which is followed by three waves that ebb, by suc-
cessive degrees, away. All this, the true rhythmical pattern,
Saintsbury's scansion effectively and completely destroys. It
forces into metre something which is basically unmetrical.

[1] ᴗ *unstressed.*   ‾ *stressed.*   ᴗ ᴗ *with medium stress.*

There is not, then, in this book any attempt at analysis of prose rhythm in the Saintsbury manner. It is assumed that prose has a 'flow' of sound, in which the falling of the stresses, the syntax, and the meaning all play a part, and which strikes upon the ear with a certain effect appropriate to the theme and purpose of the writer; and that according as it has no such recognizable 'flow' it is so much the less literature. The relationship of rhythm to the manner of writing, 'style', has been foreshadowed in previous chapters of this book; and a fairly safe, though rough, generalization can be made, which corresponds in great measure with Saintsbury's: that early prose retains something of the rhythm of verse, that prose of the middle and familiar style has the rhythm of colloquial speech, a 'prosaic' not a pronounced musical rhythm, and that some prose is so artificially wrought as to fall into the regular rhythm of verse. It is remarkable that Saintsbury himself seems to favour the prose in which there is 'method in the music'. He complains that in early eighteenth-century prose there is an 'absence of accompaniment – of sound to the sense, of music to the meaning'. Yet most critics – certainly most modern critics – would agree that prose is best when it is most truly prosaic, when it does not encroach upon the realm of verse rhythm and artifice; and we have only to turn to the *Oxford Book of English Prose*, which, like most anthologies, has a distinct partiality for the purple patch, to remind ourselves that when prose becomes 'poetic' it does almost inevitably encroach upon that realm, taking to itself at least some of the elements associated with recurrent sound. So we find ourselves back in a technical no-man's-land; or we begin to wonder again whether we are, after all, making a division where no division is.

Now that treatment of prose rhythm may well seem to be somewhat cavalier; and in a sense it is. Yet, unless we accept the analytical method of Saintsbury, and engage in his traffic with pyrrhics, amphibrachs, choriambs, and dochmiacs, there is little more to say than this, that the rhythm of prose lies in the actual syntactical structure of the sentence, the grouping of its phrases and clauses round a nucleus or predicate, with the effect now of a rising up, now of a falling away; or (more obviously) in syntactical and sense effects like climax and antithesis. And not inside the sentence only, but in the relationship of sentences to one another, of simple and multiple and complex. Prose rhythm is good and effective rather as it avoids than as it approaches verse rhythm; it has a pattern and texture of its own.

This book is mainly concerned with prose; but since rhythm enters into all expression in language, it is necessary to treat also of the rhythm of verse. At the outset, we will confine ourselves to metrical composition as Wordsworth, for example, understood it. This means that we rule out of immediate consideration not only Old English alliterative verse but also the experimental verse which is characteristic of much modern poetry. And we can have no better starting place than the stanza from Gray's *Elegy* quoted on p. 132.

> *The curfew tolls the knell of parting day,*
> *The lowing herd winds slowly o'er the lea,*
> *The ploughman homeward plods his weary way,*
> *And leaves the world to darkness and to me.*

It will be clear to the reader that the stress marks (p. 132) do not, in fact, faithfully represent the rhythm of those lines. They illustrate and exaggerate an underlying regularity, the stress falling on alternate syllables, but they do not provide for irregularity inside the regular pattern. The regularity is such that the verse can be measured into lines of a definite length in syllables; there is what may be termed a 'prevailing rhythm', but within this the falling of the stresses is variable. Moreover, there is not always, of course, the sharp black-and-white distinction between stressed (/) and unstressed; the half-stressed syllable (|) plays an important part. The rhythmical picture of that stanza would be, then, something like this:

The cùrfew tólls the knéll of pàrting dáy,
   The lowing hérd winds slowly o'er the léa,
The ploùghman homeward plóds his wéary wáy,
   And leaves the wórld to dárkness and to me.

Other readers, other scansions; but the general principle is
the same. The prevailing rhythm has a 'rising' effect – from
unstressed to stressed – in groups of chiefly two, but also of
three, or four syllables. Thus the first and the third line have
recognizably five groups of two syllables apiece, the second
and fourth three or four groups with varying numbers of
syllables. There is irregularity in regularity, or (according
as we look at it) regularity in irregularity. If we were asked
to describe technically the metrical and rhythmical pattern
of this stanza, all we could say is that it is composed of four
lines, each of ten syllables, in 'rising' rhythm of the general
type unstressed-stressed.

A prevailing rhythm based on the simple grouping unstressed-stressed is, in fact, by far the commonest in English
verse. The ballad stanza and most quatrains deriving from
it, the sonnet, decasyllabic blank verse, the rhymed (or
heroic) couplet, many special stanza forms – it is common
to all these. But unless the verse is to be monotonous with
the too regular pounding of stresses, there will be all kinds of
variations, designed to effect a perfect correspondence of
sound and sense, in the basic pattern. This can be illustrated
from the second and fourth lines already quoted. In the
second line the natural grouping is:

The lowing herd   winds slowly   o'er the léa

It is plain that the second group is, as it were, out of
step; instead of the rise (unstressed-stressed) there are two
level medium stresses (\\) followed by an unstressed
syllable that gives a falling effect. And this is precisely
what the sense demands – a pronounced drag on *winds
slow*, the adverbial syllable (*ly*) being thrown away. So,

though not for so obvious a reason, the third group in the fourth line is 'to darkness', that is to say the normal rise ('to dárk') is half balanced by a succeeding fall. Certainly, the syllables will not go into the strait-jacket of 'to dárkness and to mé', or even fit into the modified rising pattern of 'to dárkness and to mé'.

The three-syllabled group may also be the basic or prevailing element in rising rhythm, as it is, for example, in the following stanza:

> Twelve yéars have elapsed since I first took a víew
> Of my favourite field, and the bánk where they grew:
> And nòw in the gráss behóld they are láid,
> And the trée is my séat that once lént me a sháde.

Similarly, in 'falling' rhythm there are two basic groupings, one of two (stressed-unstressed) and one of three (stressed-unstressed-unstressed) syllables. Of the first Longfellow's *Hiawatha* is a notable example, though not, in one sense, a good one, since in it the stresses fall too regularly:

> Yóu shall héar how Páu-Puk-Kéewis,
> Hów the hándsome Yénadízze
> Dánced at Híawátha's wédding;
> Hów the géntle Chíbiábos,
> Hé the swéetest of musícians,
> Sáng his sóngs of lóve and lónging;
> Hów Iágoo, the gréat bóaster,
> Hé the márvellous stóry-téller,
> Tóld his táles of stránge advénture,
> That the féast might be móre jóyous,
> That the tíme might páss more gáily,
> And the guésts be móre conténted.

Of the second there are very few examples in English. One, which is often quoted and will serve as well as any, is Hood's lugubrious *Bridge of Sighs*:

> Tóuch her not scórnfully;
> Thínk of her móurnfully,
> Géntly and húmanly;
> Nót of the stáins of her,
> Áll that remáins of her
> Nów is púre wómanly.

The system of scansion, which postulates a prevailing rhythm within a variable rhythmic pattern, is based on the natural stresses of speech – what is commonly called 'speech rhythm'. Conventional scansion, deriving from a complicated metrical system in the Classical languages,[1] presupposes a formal sing-song – i.e. verse, as distinct from speech, rhythm – that can be mechanically represented, as, in fact, it is in the examples given on pp. 131–138. The four groupings, as we have called them, are called 'feet', and are classified in this way (x = unstressed):

Rising $\begin{cases} x \, / \\ xx/ \end{cases}$ iamb   adj. iambic
              anapaest   adj. anapaestic

Falling $\begin{cases} /x \\ /xx \end{cases}$ trochee   adj. trochaic
              dactyl   adj. dactylic

It is possible, therefore, once we assume a general or absolute regularity that is alien to speech, to give a formalized analysis of any piece of conventional verse.[2] Thus Gray's stanza may be technically described as consisting of four iambic pentameters, that is 'five measures of iambs', or 'five iambic feet'. There are variants of the basic feet, as for example the grouping of two equally stressed syllables

---

[1] The metrical system of Latin and Greek is based upon the quantity or length of the syllables, not on quality or stress. There is, even in English, some relationship between quality and quantity; but the subject is too difficult and too debatable a one to be discussed here.

[2] The significance of this term is made plain later in the chapter.

(//), called the spondee. Indeed, writers on the technique of verse have built up an intricate and elaborate system of English prosody ('science of versification' – COD); and to their books the interested reader is referred, especially *Historical Manual of English Prosody* by George Saintsbury, *Rhythm in English Poetry* by Sir Stanley Leathes, and *The Metres of English Poetry* by Enid Hamer.

But the approach to versification by way of natural speech rhythm has this great advantage, that it enables us to see more clearly the relationship between prose, prose form, poetry, and verse, and reminds us of the fact that metre, based on a prevailing rhythmical stress, is inherent in, not a mere external ornament of, poetic expression; and because of this it helps to explain certain developments in versification that have come to fruition in our own time. As has already been hinted, the study of the technical principles of both prose and verse tends to blunt the sharpness of a distinction which we are, perhaps, too apt to assume. There is, in fact, a common ground which waits to be explored.

However, before exploring it we have to clear the way by considering one or two artifices that are not common to prose and verse, above all rhyme. Rhyme, which came into English, through French example, in the latter part of the Middle Ages, is the most obvious of the echoic or recurrent artifices. When it is properly and effectually used, it is an integral part of the verse pattern, having a certain inevitability that makes us at once unconscious and pleasantly conscious of it; or, to put it another way, it takes its rightful place in the correspondence of sound and sense. Sometimes, though still 'inevitable', it has a heightened effect, in, for example, the heroic couplet or the final couplet of a Shakespearian sonnet, as a kind of clinching device:

> *As clocks to weight their nimble motion owe,*
> *The wheels above urg'd by the weight below:*
> *Me Emptiness, and Dulness could inspire,*
> *And were my Elasticity, and Fire.*

> *Some Daemon stole my pen (forgive th' offence)*
> *And once betrayed me into common sense:*
> *Else all my Prose and Verse were much the same;*
> *This, prose on stilts; that, poetry fall'n lame.*

> *Thus have I had thee as a dream doth flatter;*
> *In sleep, a king; but waking, no such matter.*

And now and then, as in Browning, it is so deliberately (if adroitly) accentuated as to become grotesque:

> *So munch on, crunch on, take your nuncheon,*
> *Breakfast, supper, dinner, luncheon!*
> *And just as a bulky sugar-puncheon,*
> *All ready staved, like a great sun shone . . .*

The example, however, is not quite fair. For *The Pied Piper*, from which the lines are quoted, is in, or borders on, the realm of light verse; and it is in light verse that rhyme, properly related to rhythmical and other effects, plays an outstanding part – as, for instance, in the limerick, where its presence multiples the joy:

> *There was a young woman called Starkie,*
> *Who had an affair with a darky.*
> *The result of her sins*
> *Was quadruplets, not twins –*
> *One black, and one white, and two khaki,*

and its absence delightfully points the moral:

> *There was a young man of St Bees*
> *Who was stung in the arm by a wasp;*
> *When they said, 'Does it hurt?'*
> *He replied 'No, it doesn't:*
> *It's a good job it wasn't a hornet.'*

Butler's *Hudibras* is an outstanding example of a sustained light poem in which rhyme is an effective element.

But there is another side to the picture. The necessity for

rhyming, especially according to a predetermined scheme as in a specialized stanza form, may tempt the poet into twisting a little his expression or even his sense for rhyme's sake. Keats, a slipshod and careless rhymester at the best of times, is a frequent sinner. There are two interesting examples in the ode 'To a Nightingale'. The first is in its opening lines:

> *My heart aches, and a drowsy numbness pains*
> *My sense, as though of hemlock I had drunk,*
> *Or emptied some dull opiate to the drains*
> *One minute past, and . . . Lethe-wards had sunk.*

By 'to the drains' he means, of course, 'to the dregs'; but the rhyme with *pains* has compelled him to use the word *drains* for *dregs*, and thus involved him in an ambiguous expression suggesting an incongruous image – that of a man pouring a liquid down the sink. The second occurs towards the end of the poem:

> *Thou wast not born for death, immortal bird;*
> *No hungry generations tread thee down:*
> *The voice I hear this passing night was heard*
> *In ancient days, by emperor and clown.*

Now, it is true that in Shakespeare's days 'clown' could mean 'a simple man', 'a peasant'; and it is in this sense that Keats uses it, in contrast to *emperor*. But here the word is an unnatural archaism, since *clown* in Keats's time, as now, meant something quite different, and unless the reader happens to know the older meaning the whole point of the contrast is lost. The rhyme has, in fact, blurred the sense; the reader is misled for the sake of a sound.

It is amusing to see how critics, searching for, and pretending to find, subtlety of word or image in a poem, forget that what they consider significant more often than not results from the tyranny of rhyme. There is a curious example of this in Mr John Press's *The Fire and the Fountain*. He quotes the penultimate stanza of Keats's 'Ode on Melancholy':

> *But when the melancholy fir shall fall*
>   *Sudden from heaven like a weeping cloud,*
> *That fosters the droop-headed flowers all,*
>   *And hides the green hill in an April shroud,*
> *Then glut thy sorrow on a morning rose,*
>   *Or on the rainbow of the salt-sand wave,*
>   *Or on the wealth of globed peonies;*
> *Or if thy mistress some rich anger shows,*
>   *Emprison her soft hand, and let her rave,*
>   *And feed deep, deep upon her peerless eyes.*

'We are meant,' he says gravely, '. . . to experience the full force of the word "shroud" which suggests the sadness of death implicit in the mingled sun and showers of April.' But why the sun and showers of April should suggest a shroud or imply the sadness of death is, to say the least of it, far from clear. The simpler, if more prosaic, explanation is that Keats required a rhyme for *cloud*.

That is the main charge against rhyme – that, and its fatal proneness to slip into mere vapidity:

> *. . . While they ring round the same unvaried chimes,*
> *With sure returns of still expected rhymes:*
> *Where'er you find the 'cooling western breeze'*
> *In the next line it 'whispers through the trees':*
> *If crystal streams 'with pleasing murmurs creep',*
> *The Reader's threaten'd (not in vain) with 'sleep'.*

Thomas Campion argued the matter some three hundred and fifty years ago:

> But there is yet another fault in Rhyme altogether intolerable, which is, that it enforceth a man often-times to abjure his matter and extend a short conceit beyond all bounds of art; for in quatorzains, methinks, the poet handles his subject as tyrannically as Procrustes the thief his prisoners, whom, when he had taken, he used to cast upon a bed which if they were too short to fill, he would stretch them longer, if too long, he would cut them shorter.

And Daniel, answering him, rushed to the defence:

> Nor will the general sort for whom we write (the wise
> being above books) taste these laboured measures but as
> an orderly prose when we have all done. For this kind
> acquaintance and continual familiarity ever had betwixt
> our ear and this cadence is grown to so intimate a friend-
> ship, as it will now hardly ever be brought to miss it.
> For be the verse never so good, never so full, it seems not
> to satisfy nor breed that delight, as when it is met and
> combined with a like sounding accent: which seems as the
> jointure without which it hangs loose, and cannot subsist,
> but runs wildly on, like a tedious fancy without a close.

Yet Campion, as Daniel himself admitted, wrote 'com-
mendable rhymes, which had given heretofore to the world
the best notice of his worth'. That is equally true of another
detractor, who later in the century defended the measure of
his greatest poem. Here are the opening sentences of the
note Milton prefixed to *Paradise Lost*:

> The measure is *English* Heroic Verse without Rime, as
> that of *Homer* in *Greek*, and of *Virgil* in *Latin*; Rime
> being no necessary Adjunct or true Ornament of Poem
> or good Verse, in longer Works especially, but the Inven-
> tion of a barbarous Age, to set off wretched matter and
> lame Meeter; grac'd indeed since by the use of some
> famous modern Poets, carried away by Custom, but much
> to thir own vexation, hindrance, and constraint to express
> many things otherwise, and for the most part worse then
> else they would have exprest them.

'To express many things otherwise, and for the most part
worse then else they would have exprest them.' There is the
keynote of the objection. Rhyme is apt to lead poets by the
nose. To borrow Daniel's figure, it puts their verse into a
kind of Procrustes' bed. Though, therefore, rhyme has held
its own in the poetry of the past five hundred years, there
has been from time to time a turning away from it, a declaration by precept if not in practice, of its 'inaptness in poesy'.

We have already seen how the dramatists, faced with the problem of expressing dramatic speech in verse, discarded its jingle; and Milton himself foreshadows the freeing of the longer work 'from the troublesom and modern bondage of Rimeing'. Poets have always tended to avoid this 'troublesom bondage' by allowing here and there an approximate or merely visual correspondence of sound – like, for example, *spirit – near it, wert-art-heart* in the first stanza of Shelley's *Ode to a Skylark*, or *quay-day* in Tennyson's *In Memoriam*.[1] That, however, is a mere indulgence, legitimized by custom. In modern times, especially during this century, they have tended to let the wind of rhyme blow where it listeth – that is, to break away from the patterned stanza like the sonnet and the quatrain, and to develop, both at the end of and inside the lines, sound echoes which are only partial, deliberate repetition, a system of simple or elaborate types of assonance. Here are a couple of stanzas, from Dylan Thomas, in which the half rhymes or assonances (*mister – water – enter, gravel – kennel*) are easily recognizable, and in which true rhymes fall casually (*park – dark, cup – up*) with associated sounds (*lock, ship*):

> *The hunchback in the park*
> *A solitary mister*
> *Propped between trees and water*
> *From the opening of the garden lock*
> *That lets the trees and water enter*
> *Until the Sunday sombre bell at dark*
>
> *Eating bread from a newspaper*
> *Drinking water from the chained cup*
> *That the children filled with gravel*
> *In the fountain basin where I sailed my ship*
> *Slept at night in a dog kennel*
> *But nobody chained him up.*

[1] 'As now understood in English verse, rhyme is identity of sound between words or lines extending back from the end to the last fully accented vowel & not further' – Fowler, MEU.

In general, what may be called 'straight' rhyme has given
way to a technique of sound effects within the line or
stanza, a harking back to the old alliterative measures. The
term 'technique' is used deliberately here, for repetition,
alliteration, and onomatopoeia have become basic elements
in the sound-sense pattern. Within a perfectly regular and
conventional rhyme scheme it is the technique of Gerard
Manley Hopkins:

> The world is charged with the grandeur of God.
>   It will flame out, like shining from shook foil;
>   It gathers to a greatness, like the ooze of oil
> Crushed. Why do men then now not reck his rod?
> Generations have trod, have trod, have trod;
>   And all is seared with trade; bleared, smeared with toil;
>   And wears man's smudge and shares man's smell: the soil
> Is bare now, nor can foot feel, being shod.

There a contrived and persistent alliterative and onomatopoeic echoing reinforces the meaning. It is not an artifice,
but a new way of poetic expression, avoiding rather than
emphasizing the melodious. Here is the same kind of sound-
play, without end-rhymes, in a much later poem, Stephen
Spender's *The Landscape near an Aerodrome*:

> More beautiful and soft than any moth
> With burring furred antennae feeling its huge path
> Through dusk, the air-liner with shut-off engines
> Glides over suburbs and the sleeves trailing tall
> To point the wind. Gently, broadly, she falls
> Scarcely disturbing charted currents of air.
>
> Lulled by descent, the travellers across sea
> And across feminine land indulging its easy limbs
> In miles of softness, now let their eyes trained by watching
> Penetrate through dusk the outskirts of this town
> Here where industry shows a fraying edge.
> Here they may see what is being done.

Alliteration, deliberate echo (*burring furred antennae*), assonance (*moth - path, town - done*), imperfect rhyme (*tall - falls*) are the substitutes for, or counterparts of, rhyme itself. They are part of the very texture of the verse, not something added for music's sake. Perhaps 'a new way of poetic expression' is something of an exaggeration. Shakespeare has it – 'since first your eye I eyed', 'If it were done when 'tis done then 'twere well it were done quickly', 'catch with his surcease success'; and even Keats in a trivial stumbling fashion – 'O attic shape, fair attitude . . .' But it is a kind of expression that, deriving from the past, has been developed in the present (during, that is, the past half century) as an element in colloquial poetic language, poetry in its relation to common speech. 'There are many other things to be spoken of,' says Mr Eliot, 'besides the murmur of innumerable bees or the moan of doves in immemorial elms.' This is no more than to say that in conventional verse sound effects other than rhyme are imposed musical devices, not integral but ornamental. That is true even when there is cacophony:

> *Dry clash'd his harness in the icy caves*
> *And barren chasms, and all to left and right*
> *The bare black cliff clang'd round him . . .*

When Mr Eliot says that in poetry 'dissonance, even cacophony has its place', he is not referring to this kind of deliberately designed contrast to music and melody. He means a dissonance or cacophony that is inherent in the expression, a natural (not artificial) reflection of the intermittent harshness of speech.

So, after a necessary digression, we return to rhythm. It is clear that, however much emphasis we place on speech rhythm and on scansion according to natural stresses, a vast amount of English poetry – most of the poems in *The Golden Treasury* and the *Oxford Book of Verse*, for example – does, in fact, fall into a musical or 'verse' rhythm of regular stresses, that can, in a rough and ready way, be divided into and represented as so many iambs, anapaests, trochees, and dactyls. Sometimes, in what are called lilting measures, the regularity in irregularity is obvious:

> The fields fall southward, abrupt and broken,
>   To the low last edge of the long lone land.
> If a step should sound or a word be spoken,
>   Would a ghost not rise at the strange guest's hand?
> So long have the gray bare walks lain guestless,
>   Through branches and briars if a man make way,
> He shall find no life but the sea-kind's, restless
>   Night and day.

There the prevailing rhythm of iambs and anapaests is unmistakable, though it is varied with other types of metrical feet, and the overhanging weak syllable in alternate lines making double or 'feminine' rhymes. However we scan it, it is 'singing' verse; it cannot be mistaken for prose. But sometimes, as in dramatic verse, the speech rhythm is uppermost – that is to say, the regular is, as it were, subordinated to the irregular. We have already seen that this is so, in the mediæval morality play *Everyman*, whose versifications Mr Eliot 'kept in mind' when he wrote *Murder in the Cathedral*:

> My friends, hearken what I will tell:
> I pray God reward you in his heavenly sphere.
> Now hearken, all that be here,
> For I will make my testament
> Here before you all present.
> In alms half my good I will give you with my hands twain
> In the way of charity, with good intent,
> And the other half still shall remain
> In quiet to be returned there it ought to be.

In quite another way, Shakespeare deliberately breaks the prevailing iambic of decasyllabic blank verse in his later plays by subtle variation of the caesura or pause in the line, by enjambement, and by the use of the unstressed final syllable; and as Mr J. M. Murry has pointed out, Massinger flattens out his rhythm so that his verse reads like prose:

Sir, with your pardon, I'll offer my advice. I once observed in a tragedy of ours (in which a murder was acted to the life) a guilty hearer, forced by the terror of a wounded conscience, make discovery of that which torture could not wring from him. Nor can it appear like an impossibility, but that your father, looking upon a covetous man presented on the stage, as in a mirror may see his own deformity and loathe it. Now could you but persuade the emperor to see a comedy we have that's styled *The Cure of Avarice*, and to command your father to be a spectator of it, he shall be so anatomized in the scene, and see himself so personated, the baseness of a self-torturing miserable wretch truly described, that I much hope the object will work compunction in him.

I said 'in quite another way' because, in fact, there is a basic difference between the rhythm of *Everyman* and the 'regular' prevailing rhythm that can be divided into sing-song metrical feet. For *Everyman*, though it is written in rhyme, belongs to the older tradition of alliterative verse, in which there was a fixed, or only slightly variable, number of stressed syllables to the line falling at irregular intervals, resulting therefore in a rhythm that approximates to the irregular rhythm of prose. This rhythm of stresses has always had a place in English poetry. We see, or hear it, in our last great alliterative poem, Langland's *Piers Plowman*:

For in kynde knowynge in herte   þere a myȝte begynneth
And þat falleth to the fader   þat formed vs alle,
Loked on vs with loue   and lete his sone deye
Mekely for owre mysdedes   to amende vs alle;
And ȝet wolde he hem no woo   þat wrouȝte him þat peyne,
But mekelich with mouthe   mercy bisouȝte
To haue pite of þat people   þat peyned hym to deth.[1]

[1] For in natural conscience ('knowynge in herte') a power begins, and that belongs to the Father who made us all, looked on us with love, and let His Son die meekly for our misdeeds to make us all good; and yet He wished them no woe who caused Him that pain, but meekly with his mouth he cried for mercy on them, asking God to have pity on the

It is easy to see in that short passage how the stresses are linked to the alliteration, which is itself balanced by the definite caesura in each line.

As Professor D. W. Harding points out [1] it survives in the earliest of the rhyming poets who were nevertheless striking out a basic metrical scheme. He notes how Sir Thomas Wyatt was apt to 'combine in one line two differently patterned rhythmical units which have to be held apart by a slight pause in reading', and gives by way of example:

> *Syghes are my food, drynke are my teares;*
> *Clynkinge of fetters suche musycke wolde crave;*
> *Swynke and close ayer away my lyf wears:*
> *Innocencie is all the hope I have.*
> *Rayne, wynde, or wether I judge by myne eares.*

It is common in Donne, a century or so later:

> *But I am by her death, (which word wrongs her)*
> *Of the first nothing, the Elixer grown;*
>   *Were I a man, that I were one,*
>   *I needs must know; I should preferre,*
>   *If I were any beast,*
> *Some ends, some means; Yea plants, yea stones detest,*
> *And love; All, all some properties invest;*
>   *If I an ordinary nothing were,*
>   *As shadow, a light, and body must be here.*

By that time – the end of the sixteenth century – metrical rhythm had so firmly established itself that Ben Jonson, though he rated Donne high as a poet, chides him for his irregularities. 'Donne,' he says, 'for not keeping of accent deserved hanging.' Nevertheless, the irregularly falling stress is quite common in the post-Shakespearian dramatists. We have already (pp. 147–8) noted Massinger; and in a curious early essay on *vers libre*, which will be further discussed later in this chapter, Mr T. S. Eliot instances Webster, who

---

people who did Him to death. In the original þ = modern *th*, and ȝ modern *gh*.

[1] In *The Age of Chaucer* (Penguin *Guide to English Literature I*).

'is much freer than Shakespeare', not by negligence but by design. He gives for example the famous line:

> *Cover her face; mine eyes dazzle; she died young,*

and the passage:

> *This is vain poetry; but I pray you tell me*
> *If there were proposed me, wisdom, riches, and beauty,*
> *In three several young men, which should I choose?*

It was in a similar rhythm, too, that Milton wrote *Samson Agonistes*:

> *This, this is he; softly a while,*
> *Let us not break in upon him;*
> *O change beyond report, thought, or belief!*
> *See how he lies at random, carelessly diffus'd,*
> *With languish't head unpropt,*
> *As one past hope, abandon'd*
> *And by himself given over;*
> *In slavish habit, ill-fitted weeds*
> *O'er worn and solid,*

a kind of measure which, Milton somewhat obscurely implies, is designed to be spoken rather than sung.

Perhaps it is because the tradition of metrical verse in prevailing rhythm became so firmly established in English lyrical and narrative poetry that later poets tended to think of the looser stress rhythm as something of a discovery. Coleridge, for example, has this note in his Preface to *Christabel*:

> I have only to add, that the metre of the Christabel is not, properly speaking, irregular, though it may seem so from its being founded on a new principle: namely, that of counting in each line the accents, not the syllables. Though the latter may vary from seven to twelve, yet in each line the accents will be found to be only four. Nevertheless this occasional variation in number of syllables is not introduced wantonly, or for the mere ends

of convenience, but in correspondence with some transition, in the nature of the imagery or passion.

In actual fact, the rhythmical pattern of *Christabel* does not strike us as particularly revolutionary, unless we compare it with the somewhat similar measures of Scott; nevertheless, Coleridge's 'new principle' can quite easily be recognized:

> The night is chill; the forest bare;
> Is it the wind that moaneth bleak?
> There is not wind enough in the air
> To move away the ringlet curl
> From the lovely lady's cheek –
> There is not wind enough to twirl
> The one red leaf, the last of its clan,
> That dances as often as dance it can,
> Hanging so light, and hanging so high,
> On the topmost twig that looks up at the sky.

It was left to a later poet, Gerard Manley Hopkins, to systematize this stress pattern and theorize upon it. His own descriptive analysis of what he calls 'sprung' rhythm is too technical to be quoted in any detail here. It is measured, he says, 'by feet of from one to four syllables, regularly, and for particular effects any number of weak or slack syllables may be used. It has one stress, which falls on the only syllable, if there is only one, or, if there are more, then scanning as above, on the first'. There are various refinements, such as lines that 'rove over', when the 'scanning runs on without break from the beginning, say, of a stanza to the end and all the stanza is one long strain, though written in lines asunder', and *hangers* or *outrides*, 'that is one, two, or three slack syllables added to a foot and not counting in the nominal scanning'.

To tell the truth, this elaboration of the principles of what purports to be a new metrical system, and the various diacritics which Hopkins thought it necessary to use in his verse for the guidance of the hapless reader are a much ado about nothing, the more so as Hopkins, in his theories, seems to be tied all the time to a vague quantitative conception of metre, as in Greek and Latin. That he has profoundly influenced the structure of modern verse is undeniable, not least when in his language as well as his rhythm he goes, or seems to go, to extremes:

> He leans to it, Harry bends, look. Back, elbow, and liquid
>   waist
> In him, all quail to the wallowing o' the plough: 's cheek
> crimsons; curls
> Wag or crossbridle, in a wind lifted, windlaced –
>   See his wind-lilylocks-laced;
> Churlsgrace, too, child of Amansstrength, how it hangs or
>   hurls
> Them – broad in bluff hide his frowning feet lashed! raced
> With, along them, cragiron under and cold furls –
>   With-a-fountain's shining-shot furls.

The merging and breaking of words ('Churlsgrace', 'Amansstrength', 'wind-lilylocks-laced') have become familiar devices of the modern poets, as either an aid or an adjunct to rhythmical patterns. But basically he is only substituting a sprung stress rhythm for, or imposing it upon, what he calls, somewhat ambiguously, 'running' rhythm – conventional measured verse. In a simpler way, and with less flourish of trumpets, the American poet, Walt Whitman, writing about the same time, was doing something of the same thing:

> Up through the darkness,
> While ravening clouds, the burial clouds, in black masses
>   spreading
> Lower sullen and fast athwart and down the sky,
> Amid a transparent clear belt of ether yet left in the east,
> Ascends large and calm the lord-star Jupiter,
> And nigh at hand, only a very little above,
> Swim the delicate sisters the Pleiades.

From the beach the child holding the hand of her father,
Those burial-clouds that lower victorious soon to devour all,
Watching, silently weeps.

About the same time, too, another American, Edgar Allan
Poe, was making a plea for originality in versification, the
neglect of which, he declared, was 'one of the most un-
accountable things in the world'.

So we come back to the essay of Mr Eliot, already mentioned, on *vers libre*, in which – rather naïvely – he argues
that there is no such thing as 'free' verse. 'We may,' he says,
'formulate as follows: the ghost of some simple metre
should lurk behind the arras in even the "freest" verse;
to advance menacingly as we doze, and withdraw as we
rouse. Or, freedom is only truly freedom when it appears
against the background of an artificial limitation.' However, that is neither here nor there. Mr Eliot's formula is
perfectly, even tritely, sound; it is, after all, nothing more
than a variant of the platitude that freedom is not to be
equated with licence. Certainly, as we read some modern
verse we might with reason imagine that the ghost behind
the arras had vanished altogether. But the 'background of
an artificial limitation' is there; the artifice is, indeed, more
complicated, though on the whole less disciplinary, than the
old devices of metre and rhyme. To 'scan', say, such a
passage as this, we have to forget conventional feet and
accentuation, or rather trace them faintly in a loose pattern
of recurrences and echoes:

> *You say I am repeating*
> *Something I have said before. I shall say it again.*
> *Shall I say it again? In order to arrive there,*
> *To arrive where you are, to get from where you are not,*
> *   You must go by a way wherein there is no ecstasy.*
> *In order to arrive at what you do not know*
> *   You must go by a way which is the way of ignorance.*
> *In order to possess what you do not possess*
> *   You must go by the way of dispossession.*

In order to arrive at what you are not
  You must go through the way in which you are not.
And what you do not know is the only thing you know
And what you own is what you do not own
And where you are is where you are not.

That is the later Eliot; and it is sufficient commentary on his own observation that 'this contrast between fixity and flux, this unperceived evasion of monotony, . . . is the very life of verse'. It is also, by the way, a curious reminder of the naïve belief, common in modern poets and critics, that to state a paradox in a stammering echoic idiom is to make it more profound. This particular paradox is expressed far more effectively in several passages in the Authorized Version of the Bible. 'Shall I say it again?' asks Mr Eliot; and the reader is tempted to reply, 'Certainly, provided you do not expect us to believe your saying it again signifies anything more than a mere childish juggling with words'.

2

A Note on the Syntax of Verse, and Punctuation

It is evident that the syntax of verse differs in some respects from the syntax of prose. Indeed, up to modern times there have always been certain differences of accidence. We find, for example, that Chaucer, who was writing in a period when the inflexional system was in a state of flux, often takes advantage of the fact, that a word could have two possible grammatical endings when he has to fit it into the metrical pattern of his verse. Thus the infinitive of the verb could end either in -*en* or in the weakened form -*e*. Chaucer uses it indifferently, according to his metrical requirements:

Wel koude he synge *and* pleyen *on a rote.*

The final *e* is elided before a vowel – that is, *synge* is a monosyllable. If he had written *pleye*, that also would be a monosyllable, before *on*. But metrically he requires a dissyllable here; so he writes the unabbreviated form *pleyen*:

> Wel koúde he sýnge and pléyen on a róte.

But even when the state of flux was over and such inflexions as survived were those we recognize in ordinary speech and writing today, the poet still retained certain older and archaic endings as alternatives to those established in common usage. For example, in standard English the ending of the third person singular of the verb is – (*e*)*s* – a form borrowed, by the way, from a Northern dialect; the older ending was – (*e*)*th*. In his famous sonnet *On Westminster Bridge* Wordsworth, in his first line, uses the modern form:

> *Earth* has [1] *not anything to show more fair*

And the reason is fairly obvious; if he had used the older form (*hath*), he would have been guilty of an awkward cacophony – the juxtaposition of the two *th* sounds, 'ear*th* and ha*th*'. But later on he prefers *doth* to *does* –

> *This city now doth like a garment wear*
> *The beauty of the morning.*

This time he is avoiding (as all careful poets do unless they use it deliberately for effect) the ugly sound of adjacent sibilants or *s* sounds – 'thi*s* city doe*s*'. Later still, he writes *glideth* instead of *glides* –

> *The river glideth at his own sweet will.*

Here, of course, he is satisfying the demands of metre; he requires a dissyllable ('glideth'), not a monosyllable ('glides') to suit the metrical pattern of his line. Similarly the second person singular of the personal pronoun (*thou*, *thee*, *thy*), archaic in all colloquial English but special forms of prose since the seventeenth century, is often retained in verse up to modern times, together with the appropriate verb inflection in -(*e*)*st*:

---

[1] The verbs in this and the following examples are not, of course, emphasized in the original.

> *I forgot: thou comest from thy voyage*
> *The spray is on thy face and thy hair;* [1]

and forms of the subjunctive are often used where prose
would have the indicative, especially *be* for *is*, and *were* for
was. The search for a rhyming word often forces a poet into
using archaic or unusual inflexional forms. There is an
extreme and curious example of this in Byron's *Childe
Harold's Pilgrimage* (iv, 229), where for rhyme's sake he
uses the transitive verb (*lay*) for the intransitive (*lie*):

> *And send'st him, shivering in thy playful spray*
> *And howling, to his Gods, where haply lies*
> *His petty hope in some near port or bay,*
> *And dashest him again to earth:– there let him* lay.

There is a great deal of 'wrenched' or forced syntax in the
verse of the older poets – Shakespeare, Donne, Milton, for
example; but this is paralleled by a certain looseness of
syntax in prose itself, before a more or less fixed pattern of
sentence construction in prose was established, about the
end of the seventeenth century. In general, from that time
up to the early twentieth century, verse tended to conform
to the syntax of prose, with, however, adjustments for
metrical convenience and for sound or other effects. Of
these inversion is the commonest – the alteration of the
normal order of the sentence. A remarkable example occurs
in Gray's *Elegy*:

> '*The boast of heraldry, the pomp of power,*
> *And all that beauty, all that wealth ere gave,*
> *Awaits alike th' inevitable hour*'.

Here the subject is 'th' inevitable hour', the multiple object,
making up the first two lines, preceding the (singular) verb
awaits.[2] It is unnecessary to multiply examples. They

[1] Matthew Arnold.
[2] In some texts the verb is printed *await*, it being presumed that the
sentence has the normal prose order Subject – Verb – Object. The
stanza is so rendered on the memorial to Gray adjacent to Stoke Poges
churchyard.

abound in what is now usually called 'conventional' verse, and the reason for inversion – of subject and object, for instance, or of noun and adjective – is usually apparent. In the main, it is determined by the rhythmical pattern of the line, or the exigence of rhyme, or the demands of emphasis and poetic significance. Other more subtle variations of the normal syntactical pattern often occur in the tightly-packed 'heroic' verse of the eighteenth century, especially as a means to concise balance or antithesis:

> *Feed fairer flocks, or richer fleeces shear.*
> *Now leaves the trees, and flow'rs adorn the ground.*
> *Diana Cynthus, Ceres Hybla loves.*[1]

To sum up, the normal syntactical pattern of prose is in 'conventional' verse modified by, and has imposed upon it, a pattern that depends on the technique of rhythm and on those less definable, more nebulous, effects of sound and sense that are of the very texture of poetry.

The syntax of 'unconventional' verse, sometimes called 'modern' or (usually by those who dislike it) 'modernist', has already been touched upon. It derives from the loose and mannered syntax of the older poets, and more directly from that of the experimentalists, in English and French, of the latter half of the nineteenth century. Briefly, the balance, already described, between the syntactical pattern of prose and that of conventional verse is upset in favour of one that depends upon the symbolism of words themselves, the sound and sense effects of their juxtaposition, and the demands of a new, fluid type of rhythm. The normal subject-predicate form is partially – and, in extreme examples, entirely – abandoned, together with some at least of the connectives whose function is to unite and correlate the word groups of the complex sentence. It is in the general impression, the implications and latent imagery of the words, the subtle and complicated sound echoes and effects, that the poetry lies; and to all this syntactical 'sense' is

---

[1] These examples are taken from *On the Poetry of Pope* by Geoffrey Tillotson, to which the interested reader is referred.

subordinated. The reader has, as it were, to jump innumerable ellipses, and supply what is missing by a kind of
intuition. On this Robert Bridges has an interesting note in
his edition of the poems of Gerard Manley Hopkins, the
begetter of much modern poetry. The chief cause of his
obscurity, he says, was 'his habitual omission of the
relative pronoun', as in the sentence 'O Hero savest!' for
'O Hero that savest!' 'He banished', Bridges goes on,
'these purely constructional syllables [the relative pronoun
and others] from his verse because they took up room
which he thought he could not afford them: he needed in his
scheme all his space for his poetical words, and he wished
those to crowd out every merely grammatical colourless or
toneless element.' He realized, in fact, and others after him
(usually with less native genius) realized, the dream of
C. E. Montague expressed in a passage quoted earlier on
(p. 37). But not without some inconvenience to the reader,
who not unnaturally clings to the patterns of ordinary prose.
A single example – again from Dylan Thomas – will suffice.
It is not extreme – far from it; but it will illustrate the
point:

> *It was my thirtieth year to heaven*
> *Woke to my hearing from harbour and neighbour wood*
> *And the mussel pooled and the heron*
> *Priested shore*
> *The morning beckon*
> *With water praying and call of seagull and rook*
> *And the knock of sailing boats on the net webbed wall*
> *Myself to set foot*
> *That second*
> *In the still sleeping town and set forth.*

It is reasonable to imagine that the connective *when* is
omitted after *year*, whose composite subject is made up of
the three lines beginning 'the morning beckon', *beckon*
being a noun, not a verb; that 'mussel pooled' and 'heron
priested' are adjective phrases qualifying *shore*, which would

normally be single hyphened words; and that the passage beginning 'Myself to set foot' on to the end is a verbal phrase dependent upon the main sentence. Thus the grammarian – with a sneaking fear (he confesses) that his diagnosis may be very wide of the mark. But the point is that he has no business to be diagnosing at all. The lines are intended to have a poetical significance that is only lightly related to grammatical meaning.

All this is accentuated by the entire absence of punctuation. Punctuation in prose, with its variable and changing fashions, is not within the scope of this book. It has been dealt with, once for all, briefly by Mr G. V. Carey in *Mind the Stop*, and in detail by Mr Eric Partridge in *You Have a Point There*. In general, it is related primarily to syntax and secondarily to stylistic effect. But punctuation in verse is another matter; for here rhythm also has a say. The stanza quoted from Dylan Thomas achieves its rhythmical point precisely because it is without points: that is to say, the reader is intended to be carried breathlessly on from the opening statement ('It was my thirtieth year') to the final movement or action ('and set forth'). The poet is as impatient of punctuation marks as he is of what Robert Bridges called 'constructional syllables'. There is much punctuation of the same (usually light) type in modern verse. The flow of the rhythm – untrammelled, for the most part, by conventional rhyme – tends to wash the marks away.

However, before quite recent times, when we can be tolerably sure that we have the poet's deliberate intentions represented in the text, arguments concerning punctuation are difficult and dangerous. It is reasonable to suppose that, from the late seventeenth century, the punctuation in conventional verse is more syntactical than rhythmical. In any case, unless we go to the original manuscript (in which the poet may have been merely careless), we have to depend upon the printer; and, what is more, we usually read poetry in texts prepared by editors who, rightly or wrongly, consider neither the punctuation of the manuscript nor that of the earliest printed version sacrosanct. The farther we go back the more doubtful we are, since the fashion and usage in punctuation were then noticeably different from our own. In *The Common Asphodel* Mr Robert Graves gives an interesting example from Shakespeare. He quotes side by side two texts of the sonnet 'The expense of spirit in a waste of shame' – that of the *Oxford Book of English Verse* and that of the 1609 edition of the *Sonnets*; and builds up an elaborate argument showing that the modern punctuation and spelling play havoc with the meaning, the poetic significance, as Shakespeare intended it. But his argument is of doubtful validity. Even if we could assume that the poem was printed from Shakespeare's own manuscript, we have no grounds for believing that Shakespeare followed any particular principles in, or indeed took any particular care over, his punctuation. The punctuational effects Mr Graves professes to see in the 1609 verse may, in fact, be achieved rather by luck than judgement; more especially as Shakespeare's manuscript punctuation, at any rate of the plays, is believed by scholars to have been 'often very scanty'.[1]

No doubt some poets apart from the modernists have taken particular care over punctuation, making it a real element in the syntactical and rhythmical texture of their verse. This is probably true of Milton; and it is certainly true of a lesser, but similarly learned and fastidious, poet who came long after him – A. E. Housman. 'It is best,' he wrote in the Preface to *Last Poems*, 'that what I have written should be printed while I am here to see it through the press and control its spelling and punctuation.' But we cannot get away from the fact that, unless (like Housman himself) the poet is alert and determined, the printer, following the 'style of the house', is apt to take charge. But after all, because the marks of punctuation are only conventional signs meaning different things to different readers and writers, and because, in prose as in verse, fashions in punctuation are, like other fashions, continually changing,

[1] Prof. J. Dover Wilson, in his Introduction to the Facsimile reprint of *Antony and Cleopatra*.

it is easy to over-estimate its importance and significance. Perhaps that is why the modernist poets usually reduce it to a minimum, thinking it better that the reader should have the responsibility – and the privilege – of arriving at their meaning without the doubtful and adventitious aid of commas, semi-colons, or even full stops.

CHAPTER VII

STYLE

1

IT IS TIME now to draw the threads together and consider that elusive thing which in literature, as in other expressions and activities of life, is called 'style'. At the outset we are faced, as so often, with a certain ambiguity in the meaning of the word. If, in relation to literature, we think of it as 'the manner of writing', we tend to imply a distinction between manner and matter; a distinction which, as we shall see, has some validity, but which is apt to betray us into inconsistency and confusion. In order to clarify things, then, let us go back to a fundamental question which is foreshadowed in the introductory chapter of this book: What is it that makes a piece of writing literature? It is not by any means an easy question to answer. Indeed, there is no ultimate answer, as there is no ultimate answer to such questions as 'What is love?' or even 'What is electricity?' To begin with, we have to recognize that the secret does not lie in the subject. It is easy to illustrate this by taking different translations of the same passage from another language. Thus, the story of the Good Samaritan, as it is told in the Authorized Version of the Bible is, by general consent, a piece of memorable prose. Even the slight alterations made in the Revised Version take from it something of its indefinable quality. For example, the sentence 'And in like manner a Levite also, when he came to the place, and saw him, passed by on the other side', with its syntactical complex construction in which a single main clause is modified by two adverb clauses, lacks the effect of climax achieved by the double predicate of the Authorized sentence: 'And likewise a Levite, when he was at the place, came and looked on him, and passed by on the other side.' There is, we feel (though we cannot tell precisely why), a slight falling-off from perfection. But here is the story in the well-known modern version of Dr James Moffatt:

'A man going down from Jerusalem to Jericho fell among robbers, who stripped and belaboured him and then went off, leaving him half dead. Now it so chanced that a priest was going down the same road, but on seeing him he went past on the opposite side. So did a Levite who came to the spot; he looked at him but passed on the opposite side. However a Samaritan traveller came to where he was, and felt pity when he saw him; he went to him, bound his wounds up, pouring oil and wine into them, mounted him on his own steed, took him to an inn, and attended to him. Next morning he took out a couple of shillings and gave them to the innkeeper, saying, "Attend to him, and if you are put to any extra expense, I will refund you on my way back".'

Of that we should say that it is a competent piece of prose – no more. It has nothing of the memorableness of literature. The same facts are there and the same characters doing the same things; but the inward 'life' of the narrative has gone. Admittedly, the comparison is not quite fair, since we are considering English written in two different idioms that are dependent on time – a point which is discussed later in this chapter. But the central fact remains, that the same story told in one way is literature, and told in another is not.

This question of the relationship of matter and manner arises in a special way whenever literature is closely associated with the kind of writing which is common to us all – the letter, and (to a less extent) the journal or diary. We all write letters to friends and acquaintances, giving the news and commenting on this and that; and some of us record in a notebook our doings from day to day. But these letters and diaries, however interesting to our correspondents or to those whom we allow to peep into them, do not of themselves become literature. Yet some people, not in the ordinary sense 'writers', have somehow worked a transformation in the everyday language of private communication, so that it has the quality of permanence. Here is Dorothy Osborne writing to her lover, Sir William Temple, about the middle of the seventeenth century:

When I have supped I go into the garden, and so to the side of a small river that runs by it, where I sit down and wish you with me (you had best say this is not kind, neither). In earnest, it is a pleasant place, and would be more so to me if I had your company, as I sit there sometimes till I am lost with thinking; and were it not for some cruel thoughts of the crossness of my fortune, that will not let me sleep there, I should forget there were such a thing to be done as going to bed. Since I writ this, my company is increased by two, my brother Harry, and a fair niece, my brother Peyton's daughter. She is so much a woman that I am almost ashamed to say I am her aunt, and so pretty, that if I had any design to gain a servant I should not like her company; but I have none, and therefore I shall endeavour to keep her here as long as I can persuade her father to spare her, for she will easily consent to it, having so much of my humour (though it be the worst thing in her) as to like a melancholy place, and little company. . . . My father is reasonably well, but keeps his chamber still; but will hardly, I am afraid, ever be so perfectly recovered as to come abroad again.

And here is Lady Mary Wortley Montague writing home from her travels:

Apropos of distempers, I am going to tell you a thing that I am sure will make you wish yourself here. The small-pox, so fatal, and so general amongst us, is here entirely harmless by the invention of ingrafting, which is the term they give it. There is a set of old women who make it their business to perform the operation every autumn, in the month of September, when the great heat is abated. People send to one another to know if any of their family has a mind to have the small-pox: they make parties for this purpose, and when they are met (com-

monly fifteen or sixteen together), the old woman comes
with a nut-shell of the matter of the best sort of small-pox,
and asks what veins you please to have opened. She immediately rips open that you offer to her with a large
needle (which gives you no more pain than a common
scratch), and puts into the vein as much venom as can lie
upon the head of her needle, and after binds up the little
wound with a hollow bit of shell; and in this manner opens
four or five veins. Every year thousands undergo this
operation; and the French ambassador says pleasantly,
that they take the small-pox here by way of diversion, as
they take the waters in other countries. There is no
example of anyone that has died in it; and you may
believe I am very well satisfied of the safety of this experiment, since I intend to try it on my dear little son.

And here, most familiarly, is Pepys, writing up his Diary for
the tenth of February, 1663–4:

10th. By coach to my Lord Sandwich, to his new house,
a fine house, but deadly dear, in Lincoln's Inne Fields,
where I found and spoke a little to him. He is high and
strange still, but did ask me how my wife did, and at
parting remembering him to his cozen. My wife abroad
to buy Lent provisions. I did give my wife's brother 10s.
and a coat that I had by me, a close-bodied, light-coloured
coat, with a gold edgeing in each seam, that was the lace
of my wife's best pettycoat, that she had when I married
her. He is going into Holland to seek his fortune. My pain
do leave me without coming to any great excess; but my
cold that I had got I suppose was not very great, it being
only the leaving of my waste-coate unbuttoned one
morning.

Even when we have allowed for an intrinsic or historical or
even sentimental interest in these passages, we are still
conscious of something in the language which lifts it above
the English of every day. Briefly, it is this: they discovered
for their personal thoughts, addressed in the first place to a

particular person (in Pepys's case presumably himself) a freshness of expression, a peculiar aptness and directness of word and phrase, which give to their prose the effect of animated speech. It is not unreasonable to say that their writing is, as far as any writing can be, spontaneous and artless. The matter finds its own manner, as water finds its own level. They write, according to the idiom of their time, sometimes using a loose syntax of their own, in what may be termed a natural style.

It is out of this natural style, rooted in speech, that (as I have shown in *The Pattern of English*) there developed the normal texture of English prose. Before the closing years of the seventeenth century, the time of Dryden, the gap between speech and formal as distinct from personal writing was – except in the prose of the drama – a wide one. From this not even Bunyan's prose can be excepted, for though he introduced into it many sturdy colloquialisms, it follows in its vocabulary, imagery, and to some extent the pattern of its sentences a literary model – the Authorized Version of the Bible. Hazlitt termed this 'norm', as it may be called, 'familiar style'.[1] 'To write a genuine familiar of truly English style,' he says, 'is to write as anyone would speak in common conversation who had a thorough command and choice of words, or who could discourse with ease, force, and perspicuity, setting aside all pedantic and oratorical flourishes.' That, as we have already seen, has some bearing on the recording of actual speech in the novel and the play. Hazlitt, however, is speaking not of this, but of narrative and expository prose. Familiar style, he says, 'is employed as an unvarnished medium to convey ideas'. It is a formal artistic counterpart, and indeed development, of the personal artless style. The writer trims his sentences to an accepted syntactical pattern, subject and predicate with the modification of clause and phrase, filling up the common ellipses of the spoken word; suggests by turns of expression the emphases and gestures of ordinary talk; uses a vocabu-

---

[1] It, or something corresponding to it, is often called 'the middle style' nowadays.

lary that is at once intelligible, interesting, and evocative; and so varies his constructions that he avoids the effect of monotony. He gives coherence to speech, at the same time retaining certain of its characteristics. His immediate appeal is through the eye of the reader; but he does not forget the reader's ear.

'An unvarnished medium to convey ideas.' It is the prose we are most accustomed to, because it is the prose that, on a lower level, we ordinarily write. We should expect to find it, as Hazlitt suggests, in the literature 'conveying ideas', in criticism, in biography, in the factual (for example, the scientific) account and commentary, in philosophical writing, in books of history, and in the essay. Here, from the kind of literature specified, are half a dozen representative examples:

'As for Jonson, to whose character I am now arrived, if we look upon him while he was himself (for his last plays were but his dotages), I think him the most learned and judicious writer which any theatre ever had. He was a most severe judge of himself, as well as others. One cannot say he wanted wit, but rather that he was frugal of it. In his works you find little to retrench or alter. Wit, and language, and humour also in some measure, we had before him; but something of art was wanting to the drama, till he came. He managed his strength to more advantage than any who preceded him. You seldom find him making love in any of his scenes, or endeavouring to move the passions; his genius was too sullen and saturnine to do it gracefully, especially when he knew he came after those who had performed both to such a height. Humour was his proper sphere; and in that he was delighted most to represent mechanic people.

John Dryden: *Essay of Dramatic Poesy*.

In Poetry they must be allowed to excel all other Mortals; wherein the Justness of their Similes, and the minuteness, as well as Exactness of their Descriptions, are indeed inimitable. Their Verses abound very much in both of these; and usually contain either some exalted

Notions of Friendship and Benevolence, or the Praises of those who were Victors in Races, and other bodily Exercises. Their Buildings, although very rude and simple, are not inconvenient, but well contrived to defend them from all Injuries of Cold and Heat. They have a Kind of Tree, which at Forty Years old loosens in the Root, and falls with the first Storm; it grows very strait, and being pointed like Stakes with a sharp Stone, (for the Houyhnhnms know not the use of Iron) they stick them erect in the Ground about ten Inches asunder, and then weave in Oat-straw, or sometimes Wattles betwixt them. The Roof is made after the same Manner, and so are the Doors.

Jonathan Swift: Gulliver's Travels.

In our return home we met with a very odd accident; which I cannot forbear relating, because it shows how desirous all who know Sir Roger are of giving him marks of their esteem. When we were arrived upon the verge of his estate, we stopped at a little inn to rest ourselves and our horses. The man of the house had, it seems, been formerly a servant in the knight's family; and to do honour to his old master, had some time since, unknown to Sir Roger, put him up in a sign-post before the door; so that the knight's head hung out upon the road about a week before he himself knew anything of the matter. As soon as Sir Roger was acquainted with it, finding that his servant's indiscretion proceeded wholly from affection and goodwill, he only told him that he had made him too high a compliment; and when the fellow seemed to think that could hardly be, added with a more decisive look, that it was too great an honour for any man under a duke; but told him at the same time, that it might be altered with a very few touches, and that he himself would be at the charge of it.

Joseph Addison: The Spectator.

Still, in full measure, the sense of creative activity belongs only to genuine creation; in literature we must never forget that. But what true man of letters ever can forget it? It is no such common matter for a gifted nature to come into possession of a current of true and living ideas, and to produce amidst the inspiration of them, that we are likely to under-rate it. The epochs of Aeschylus and Shakespeare make us feel their pre-eminence. In an epoch like those is, no doubt, the true life of a literature; there is the promised land, towards which criticism can only beckon. That promised land it will not be ours to enter, and we shall die in the wilderness: but to have desired to enter it, to have saluted it from afar, is already, perhaps, the best distinction among contemporaries; it will certainly be the best title to esteem with posterity.

One day, a little time after they had come back to Orchard Side, a neighbour arrived with a tame hare he thought Cowper might like to keep as a pet. He was delighted with it. For hours every day he would watch its antics and try to tame it. The good people of Olney, delighted that something had at last given pleasure to the poor gentleman at Orchard Side, all began to give him hares. This was too much of a good thing. Cowper thanked them all with his usual politeness, but only kept three of their presents. For the next few years these hares – Bess, Puss and Tiny – were a dominating interest in his life. His sympathy had always enabled him to enter into the lives of those he saw around him. And with the hares he had entered into a life from which all the painful problems of human existence were necessarily absent. In their company he escaped for a moment from hell – not into heaven, but into Eden before the Fall; into a life physical and sylvan, innocent of the knowledge of good and evil; a remote Hans Andersen garden world, where a blade of grass was as big as a bush and the greatest enemy was a hornet and the garden wall was the end of the cosmos.

Lord David Cecil: *The Stricken Deer*.

An examination of Aristotle's Law of Gravitation exemplifies this abstractive process inherent in science. The Law involves a classification of the things around us. There are the heavy bodies with the property of tending downwards, and there are the other elements such as flames, with the intrinsic nature that they tend upwards though they are component things on the earth's surface. These upward moving things tend to their proper place, which is the heavens. The stars and planets form yet a third class of things which by their own nature are in the heavens, things which are ingenerable and incorruptible. In this classification of the components of physical nature yet a fourth component remains over, in its character unique and thus the only member of its class. This component is the Earth, the centre of the Universe, by reference to which all these other types of being are defined.

Alfred North Whitehead: *Adventures of Ideas*.

Now, if we subject these passages to aesthetic literary criticism (which this book does not pretend to do), we find differences between them, individualities of expression, turns of phrase or sentence characteristic to the several authors, vocabulary that varies with the subject treated. But in technique, in the actual syntax and construction of the sentences, and in their relationship to one another, they have a common factor. They are representative of what we justly and commonly think of as English 'prose'. When we read them we are not conscious of abnormality or eccentricity because they follow a pattern that, having established itself in common usage, we recognize at once in literature. They are written, that is, in 'familiar' style – and the term 'familiar' has here a double significance.

But the postulation (a trifle arbitrary, it may be) of a norm or standard implies a departure from it. To begin with, the early prose, which precedes the evolution of the familiar style, has characteristics of its own. This is, in part, a matter of syntax, as I have shown in *The Pattern of English*; but it also arises from the fact that such prose was, in the main, divorced from speech. It has a literary rather than a col-loquial background – the background of the classical (Greek and Latin) vocabulary and a sentence structure that, natural to an inflected, was unnatural to an uninflected language. This kind of writing, usually on a high and noble theme, is familiar in the prose of Milton and Sir Thomas Browne; its characteristics are 'the rolling period, the stately epithet, the noun rich in poetic associations, the subordinate clauses that give the sentence weight and significance, the grandeur like that of wave following wave in the open sea'. This, however, takes us into another region, which is explored later. So, too, does the Authorized Version of the Bible. But this separation from the manner of speech, emphasized and perhaps exaggerated for us by changes in the language which have occurred since, is also apparent in less august prose of the early period. Here, for example, is Sir Philip Sidney in the *Apologie for Poetrie*:

> The incomparable *Lacedemonians* did not only carry that kinde of Musicke ever with them to the field; but even at home, as such songs were made, so were they all content to bee the singers of them, when the lusty men were to tell what they dyd, the olde men what they had done, and the young men what they wold doe. And where a man may say, that *Pindar* many times prayseth highly victories of small moment, matters rather of sport then vertue: as it may be aunswered, it was the fault of the Poet, and not of the Poetry; so indeede the chiefe fault was in the tyme and custome of the Greekes, who set those toyes at so high a price, that *Phillip* of *Macedon* reckoned a horserace wonne at *Olympus* among hys three fearefull felicities. But as the unimitable *Pindar* often did, so is that kinde most capable and most fit to awake the thoughts from the sleep of idleness, to imbrace honorable enterprises.

It is interesting to compare this passage with its colourful vocabulary, ('lusty men', 'fearefull felicities', 'imbrace honorable enterprises'), its loose periodic sentences, and its artful comparisons, with that quoted from Dryden on p. 96. Elizabethan translations are couched in the same kind of exalted language, the heritage of a classical tradition and a liberal scholarship. A passage from Florio's translation of Montaigne's *Essaies* will serve for illustration:

> If a man urge me to tell wherefore I loved him, I feel it cannot be expressed, but by answering; Because it was he, because it was myself. There is beyond all my discourse, and besides what I can particularly report of it, I know not what inexplicable and fatal power, a mean and Mediatrix of this indissoluble union. We sought one another before we had seen one another, and by the reports we heard one of another; which wrought a greater violence in us, than the reason of reports may well bear; I think by some secret ordinance of the heavens we embraced one another by our names. And at our first meeting, which was by chance at a great feast, and solemn meeting of a whole township, we found ourselves so surprised, so known, so acquainted, and so combinedly bound together, that from thenceforward nothing was so near unto us as one unto another.

There is little in that to foreshadow the familiar style that characterized the essay, for the most part, in later years – a literary form in which Addison sought to bring 'philosophy out of closets and libraries, schools and colleges, to dwell in clubs and assemblies, at tea-tables and in coffee-houses'. Even when Bacon introduced it into English, he used a written, rather than a familiar, language, a language which in its aphoristic conciseness and balanced construction goes back to the Latin:

> *Reuenge* is a kinde of Wilde Iustice; which the more Mans Nature runs to, the more ought Law to weed it out. For as for the first Wrong, it doth but offend the Law; but the *Reuenge* of that wrong, putteth the Law out of Office. Certainly, in taking *Reuenge*, A Man is but euen

with his Enemy; But in passing it ouer, he is Superiour: For it is a Princes part to Pardon. And *Salomon*, I am sure, saith, *It is the glory of a Man to passe by an offence.* That which is past, is gone, and Irrevocable; And wise Men haue Enough to doe, with things present, and to come: Therefore, they doe but trifle with themselues, that labour in past matters. There is no man, doth a wrong, for the wrongs sake; But therby to purchase himselfe, Profit, or Pleasure, or Honour, or the like. Therfore why should I be angry with a Man, for louing himselfe better than mee? And if any Man should doe wrong, meerely out of ill nature, why? yet it is but like the Thorn, or Bryar, which prick, and scratch, because they can doe no other.

It may be, of course, that – as some maintain – the language of the sixteenth- and seventeenth-century writers is nearer to speech than we are apt to imagine. If that is so, we are only driven back to the conclusion that then, as later, the written word marched with the spoken word, and that we imagine a gap only because we have but scanty knowledge of actual conversation some four centuries ago. But the point is an academic one. The change in the texture of prose is still there.

It is evident that within the norm there are all kinds of variations. A writer, conforming to the familiar style in essay, biography, or treatise, nevertheless stamps it with his own signature. Sometimes this signature is so pronounced that his prose achieves a pattern of its own, easily recognizable as something apart from the normal. It is, for example, in the essays of Charles Lamb, who deliberately went back to the vocabulary and style of the older writers, and evolved a peculiar technique of parenthesis and digression to give the effect of talk – something akin to the 'stream-of-consciousness' method already noted in the novel:

> I like to meet a sweep – understand me – not a grown sweeper – old chimney-sweepers are by no means attractive – but one of those tender novices, blooming through their first nigritude, the maternal washings not quite

effaced from the cheek – such as come forth with the dawn, or somewhat earlier, with their little professional notes sounding like the *peep peep* of a young sparrow; or liker to the matin lark should I pronounce them, in their aerial ascents not seldom anticipating the sunrise?

I have a kindly yearning toward these dim specks – poor blots – innocent blacknesses –

I reverence these young Africans of our own growth – these almost clergy imps, who sport their cloth without assumption; and from their little pulpits (the tops of chimneys), in the nipping air of a December morning, preach a lesson of patience to mankind.

Of this style Lamb himself said – speaking, perhaps, with his tongue in his cheek – that it was 'crude, unlicked, villainously pranked in an affected array of antique modes and phrases'. But we know, and he knew, that there is more in it than this. An examination candidate whose paper I had the fortune or misfortune to assess, faced with the formidable task of commenting on Lamb's self judgement, gave him the lie direct: 'Lamb had a completely matured or "licked" style'. Out of the mouths of babes and sucklings . . .

So it is in Carlyle, who developed a Germanic turn of sentence, hurling imperatives, rhetorical questions, italics for emphasis, and detached observations at the unfortunate reader:

Poor Cromwell, – great Cromwell! The inarticulate Prophet; Prophet who could not speak. Rude, confused, struggling to utter himself, with his savage depth, with his wild sincerity; and he looked so strange, among the elegant Euphemisms, dainty little Falklands, didactic Chillingworths, diplomatic Clarendons! Consider him. An outer hull of chaotic confusion, visions of the Devil, nervous dreams, almost semi-madness; and yet such a clear determinate man's-energy working in the heart of that. A kind of chaotic man. The ray as of pure starlight and fire, working in such an element of boundless hypochondria, unformed black of darkness! And yet withal this hypochondria, what was it but the very greatness of the man? The depth and tenderness of his wild affections: the quantity of sympathy he had with things, – the quantity of insight he would yet get into the heart of things, the mastery he would yet get over things: this was his hypochondria. The man's misery, as man's misery always does, came of his greatness. Samuel Johnson too is that kind of man. Sorrow-stricken, half-distracted; the wide element of mournful black enveloping him, – wide as the world. It is the character of a prophetic man; a man with his whole soul seeing, and struggling to see . . .

But the familiar style is, as Hazlitt suggested, characteristic of that prose which 'conveys ideas', which states facts and gives a commentary upon them, which expresses critical opinion; of the prose which is in the good sense of the word 'prosaic' – 'proper words in the proper order'.

2

But that, after all, is not all. This 'prosaic' prose, in its form, mode of expression, and vocabulary affords satisfaction and gives pleasure to the mind and intellect. There is, however, also a prose that reaches out to the heart or the emotions; and such prose has something of the quality of poetry. Once again we are driven back to the relationship of matter and manner. Whenever the writer rises (in Milton's phrase) to the 'hight of his great argument', or when through the medium of words, he has, for example, to depict the colour of a natural scene, his prose is quickened to match the subject. In this process of quickening there are several elements, the chief of which are the use of vocabulary and image, and the achievement of a certain rhythm in the construction of the sentences and their relationship to one another, of which more is said later. But if this prose, in a measure taking to itself wings, is nevertheless to remain prose, the correspondence of matter and manner must be absolute. It must arise naturally, and have the mark of sincerity; it must justify itself to the reader. Otherwise it becomes mere ornamental verbiage, or, worse still, degenerates into a mongrel form, neither poetry nor prose.

Now, much of the older prose had of itself this poetic character, for it still retains something of the spirit and even the form of that poetry with which all literature begins. This is, in fact, only another way of saying that it had not yet achieved the familiar style. A few examples of it, from Sir Thomas Browne, from Sidney, and from Florio have already been quoted, to illustrate other points, in the pages of this book. It was of this kind of prose that Mr Somerset Maugham was speaking in the quotation given on p. 31. In the same paragraph he observes of the prose of Sir Thomas Browne that when, in the last chapter of *Hydriotaphia*, he is writing on a high theme, the destiny of man, 'the matter wonderfully fits the baroque splendour of the language', but when, early in the book, he describes the findings of the burial urns 'in the same splendid manner, the effect is less happy'. In actual fact, Mr Maugham's statement is open to question; and since that has a bearing on the general argument advanced in this section, two relevant passages are quoted:

But the iniquity of oblivion blindly scattereth her poppy, and deals with the memory of men without distinction to merit of perpetuity. Who can but pity the founder of the pyramids? Herostratus lives that burnt the temple of Diana, he is almost lost that built it. Time hath spared the epitaph of Adrian's horse, confounded that of himself. In vain we compute our felicities by the advantage of our good names, since bad have equal durations, and Thersites is like to live as long as Agamemnon without the favour of the everlasting register. Who knows whether the best of men be known, or whether there be not more remarkable persons forgot, than any that stand remembered in the known account of time? The first man had been unknown as the last, and Methuselah's long life had been his only chronicle.

In a field of Old Walsingham, not many months past, were digged up between forty and fifty urns, deposited in a dry and sandy soil, not a yard deep, nor far from one another. – Not all strictly of one figure, but most answering these described; some containing two pounds of bones, distinguishable in skulls, ribs, jaws, thigh bones, and teeth, with fresh impressions of their combustion; besides the extraneous substances, like pieces of small boxes, or combs handsomely wrought, handles of small brass instruments, brazen nippers, and in one some kind of opal.

It is evident that the sombre dignity of the immediate subject, the indiscriminating oblivion that overtakes all mortal things, has itself kindled and enriched the prose of the first passage, and that the prose of the second, though it is by no means in the familiar style, is more 'prosaic', since it is more closely tied to factual narrative. There is a closer alliance of matter and manner than Mr Maugham appears to suggest; the prose rises to the 'poetic' when there is an underlying poetry in the theme that inspires it. Or let us take an example of another kind. When, in the *Essays*, Bacon writes on political or philosophical or worldly-wise subjects, his prose, however individual in texture, has the qualities that belong to an exalted rather than a familiar style. Of that the passage quoted on pp. 172–3 is sufficient example. But when, as in the essay 'Of Gardens', he slips into natural description, it takes on a kind of lyrical note in its vocabulary and turns of phrase:

And because, the *Breath* of Flowers, is farre Sweeter in the Aire, (where it comes and Goes, like the Warbling of Musick) then in the hand, therfore nothing is more fit for that delight, then to know, what be the *Flowers*, and *Plants*, that doe best perfume the Aire. Roses Damask & Red, are fast Flowers of their Smels; So that; you may walke by a whole Row of them, and finde Nothing of their Sweetnesse; Yea though it be, in a Mornings Dew. Bayes likewise yeeld no Smell, as they grow. Rosemary

little; Nor Sweet-Marioram. That, which aboue all
Others, yeelds the *Sweetest Smell* in the *Aire*, is the Violet;
Specially the White-double-Violet, which comes twice a
Yeare; About the middle of *Aprill*, and about *Bartholo-
mew-tide*.

Again, matter and manner correspond; the flowers have cast
a spell upon the prose itself.

It is necessary here to digress into a brief consideration of
the prose of the Authorized Version of the Bible, since that
is by far the best-known example of our early prose, and
has led to a certain confusion of thought and terms that need
some clarification. The subject is discussed, from the syntactical point of view, in *The Pattern of English*. All that
needs to be said here is: first, that many passages in the
Old Testament and two or three in the New are translations
of Hebrew and Greek poems, and retain in what is outwardly prose form something of the verse rhythm (as, for
example, Hebrew parallelism) of the originals; second, that
the essential poetic, pictorial imagery of Hebrew prose is
reflected in that of the Old Testament, and in the New,
where the original is more colloquial and less colourful, the
prose has a curious emotive power because it is couched (as,
indeed, it is in the Old) in an idiom that was already archaic
when the translation was made. Here, by way of example,
is a piece of prose narrative that, translated as it is from a
primitive original into a 'heightened' English form, possesses
that 'poetic' quality which is characteristic of the Authorized
Version:

And Jael went out to meet Sisera, and said unto him,
Turn in, my lord, turn in to me; fear not. And when he
had turned in unto her into the tent, she covered him with
a mantle. And he said unto her, Give me, I pray thee, a
little water to drink; for I am thirsty. And she opened a
bottle of milk, and gave him drink, and covered him.
Again he said unto her, Stand in the door of the tent, and
it shall be, when any man doth come and enquire of thee,
and say, Is there any man here? that thou shalt say, No.

Then Jael Heber's wife took a nail of the tent, and took an hammer in her hand, and went softly unto him, and smote the nail into his temples, and fastened it into the ground: for he was fast asleep and weary. So he died.

And here is the English rendering of the Hebrew poem which recounted that grim episode:

Blessed above women shall Jael the wife of Heber the Kenite be, blessed shall she be above women in the tent. He asked water, and she gave him milk; she brought forth butter in a lordly dish. She put her hand to the nail, and her right hand to the workmen's hammer; and with the hammer she smote Sisera, she smote off his head, when she had pierced and stricken through his temples. At her feet he bowed, he fell, he lay down: at her feet he bowed, he fell: where he bowed, there he fell down dead.

It is easy to see (and hear) that this passage has a different texture and spirit. However much we may be led astray by its form in the Authorized Version, we cannot but feel that it is poetry.[1] The larger question of poetry in other than

[1] The preservation, in part, of the Hebrew metrical form, in which phrases parallel, or echo one another, is seen if the passage is printed like this:

Blessed above women shall Jael the wife of Heber the Kenite be,
Blessed shall she be above women in the tent.

He asked water,
And she gave him milk;
She brought forth butter in a lordly dish.
She put her hand to the nail,
And her right hand to the workmen's hammer;
And with the hammer she smote Sisera,
She smote off his head,
When she had pierced and stricken through his temples.
At her feet he bowed,
He fell,
He lay down:
At her feet he bowed,
He fell:
Where he bowed,
There he fell down dead.

Biblical prose, which raises difficult problems in literary definition, is discussed later (section 3).

To return, however, to what (for want of a better term) we have called 'poetic' or 'emotive' prose. It is no contradiction or paradox that this arises naturally and, indeed, inevitably out of the familiar style when the theme demands it; when, that is, the writer is urged into exalted, or moving, or pictorial expression by the very nature of what he has to say. A brief annotated anthology will illustrate this:

1 (*a*) In this work, when it shall be found that much is omitted, let it not be forgotten that much likewise is performed; and though no book was ever spared out of tenderness to the author, and the world is little solicitous to know whence proceeded the faults of that which it condemns; yet it may gratify curiosity to inform it, that the *English Dictionary* was written with little assistance of the learned, and without any patronage of the great; not in the soft obscurities of retirement, or under the shelter of academick bowers, but amidst inconvenience and distraction, in sickness and in sorrow. It may repress the triumph of malignant criticism to observe, that if our language is not here fully displayed, I have only failed in an attempt which no human powers have hitherto completed. I have protracted my work till most of those whom I wished to please have sunk into the grave, and success and miscarriage are empty sounds: I therefore dismiss it with frigid tranquillity, having little to fear or hope from censure or from praise.

Samuel Johnson: Preface to the Dictionary.

(*b*) I have presumed to mark the moment of conception: I shall now commemorate the hour of my final deliverance. It was on the day, or rather night, of the 27th of June 1787, between the hours of eleven and twelve, that I wrote the last lines of the last page, in a summer-house in my garden. After laying down my pen, I took several turns in a *berceau*, or covered walk of acacias, which commands a prospect of the country, the lake, and the mountains. The air was temperate, the sky was serene, the silver orb of the moon was reflected from the waters, and all nature was silent. I will not dissemble the first emotions of joy on the recovery of my freedom, and, perhaps, the establishment of my fame. But my pride was soon humbled, and a sober melancholy was spread over my mind, by the idea that I had taken an everlasting leave of an old and agreeable companion, and that whatsoever might be the future date of my History, the life of the historian must be short and precarious.

Edward Gibbon: *Memoirs*.

These two passages are not quite fair examples, since both Johnson and Gibbon were writers who, in their vocabulary and sentence structure, ordinarily departed somewhat from the 'familiar' and affected what is sometimes called the 'grand' style – Gibbon with the rise and fall of his dignified sentences that suit the march of his history, and Johnson with his classical vocabulary (though this element in his prose is often exaggerated) and sounding antithesis. However, they will serve, as showing, paradoxically, that the grand style can be exalted by allying and in some measure subordinating its characteristics to a certain direct simplicity of diction with which both writers express, naturally and unconsciously, a personal emotion. The occasion, and the theme of ultimate fulfilment inspire a kind of prose in which fact is transformed into something more than fact.

2 Though I have now travelled the *Sussex-downs* upwards of thirty years, yet I still investigate that chain of majestic mountains with fresh admiration year by year; and think I see new beauties every time I traverse it. Perhaps I may be singular in my opinion, and not so happy as to convey to you the same idea; but I never contemplate these mountains without thinking I perceive somewhat analogous to growth in their gentle swellings and smooth fungus-like protuberances, their fluted sides,

and regular hollows and slopes, that carry at once the air
of vegetative dilatation and expansion . . .

. . . Or was there ever a time when these immense
masses of calcarious matter were thrown into fermentation by some adventitious moisture; were raised and
leavened into such shapes by some plastic power; and so
made to swell and heave their broad backs into the sky
so much above the less animated clay of the wild below?
          Gilbert White: *The Natural History of Selborne*.

There are passages in the *Selborne* that are more lyrical
than this; but this is a remarkable example of the alliance of
matter with manner. White, lost in his admiration of this
'chain of majestic mountains', suddenly takes to moun-
tainous words – *protuberances, vegetative, dilatation, calcarious, fermentation, adventitious*; and the general effect is
not turgid, but curiously poetic, the piling up of syllables
corresponding with the piling up of the 'calcarious matter'
that forms the downs themselves.

3 (*a*) Chivalry was dying; the abbey and the castle were
soon together to crumble into ruins; and all the forms,
desires, beliefs, convictions of the old world were passing
away, never to return. A new continent had risen up
beyond the western sea. The floor of heaven, inlaid with
stars, had sunk back into an infinite abyss of immeasur-
able space; and the firm earth itself, unfixed from its
foundations, was seen to be but a small atom in the awful
vastness of the universe. In the fabric of habit in which
they had so laboriously built for themselves, mankind
were to remain no longer.

And now it is all gone – like an unsubstantial pageant
faded; and between us and the old English there lies a
gulf of mystery which the prose of the historian will never
adequately bridge. They cannot come to us, and our
imagination can but feebly penetrate to them. Only
among the aisles of our cathedrals, only as we gaze upon
their silent figures sleeping on their tombs, some faint

conceptions float before us of what these men were when they were alive; and perhaps in the sound of church bells, that peculiar creation of mediæval age, which falls upon the ear like the echo of a vanished world.

J. A. Froude: *History of England.*

(*b*) No, we are all seekers still! seekers often make mistakes, and I wish mine to redound to my own discredit only, and not to touch Oxford. Beautiful city! so venerable, so lovely, so unravaged by the fierce intellectual life of our century, so serene!

'*There are our young barbarians all at play!*'

And yet, steeped in sentiment as she lies, spreading her gardens to the moonlight, and whispering from her towers the last enchantments of the Middle Age, who will deny that Oxford, by her ineffable charm, keeps ever calling us nearer to the true goal of all of us, to the ideal, to perfection, – to beauty, in a word, which is only truth seen from another side? – nearer, perhaps, than all the science of Tubingen. Adorable dreamer, whose heart has been so romantic! who hast given thyself so prodigally, given thyself to sides and to heroes not mine, only never to the Philistines! home of lost causes, and forsaken beliefs, and unpopular names, and impossible loyalties! Apparitions of a day, what is our puny warfare against the Philistines, compared with the warfare which this queen of romance has been waging against them for centuries, and will wage after we are gone?

Matthew Arnold: *Essays in Criticism.*

Behind both passages is the sense of historical time, a sense which inspires Froude to an evocative recital of the tokens of a vanishing and vanished world, Arnold to a form of prose that abandoning the syntax of ordinary statement, passes into rhetorical question and apostrophe.

4 (*a*) Guns which were heard at Brussels were ploughing up their ranks, and comrades falling, and the resolute

survivors closing in. Towards evening, the attack of the French, repeated and resisted so bravely, slackened in its fury. They had other foes besides the British to engage, or were preparing for a final onset. It came at last: the columns of the Imperial Guard marched up the hill of St Jean, at length and at once to sweep the English from the height which they had maintained all day, and spite of all: unscared by the thunder of the artillery, which hurled death from the English line – the dark rolling column pressed on and up the hill. It seemed almost to crest the eminence, when it began to wave and falter. Then it stopped, still facing the shot. Then at last the English troops rushed from the post from which no enemy had been able to dislodge them, and the Guard turned and fled.

No more firing was heard at Brussels – the pursuit rolled miles away. Darkness came down on the field and city: and Amelia was praying for George, who was lying on his face, dead, with a bullet through his heart.

W. M. Thackeray: *Vanity Fair*.

(*b*) The second mast was yet standing, with the rags of a rent sail, and a wild confusion of broken cordage flapping to and fro. The ship had struck once, the same boatman hoarsely said in my ear, and then lifted in and struck again. I understood him to add that she was parting amidships, and I could readily suppose so, for the rolling and beating were too tremendous for any human work to suffer long. As he spoke, there was another cry of pity from the beach; four men arose with the wreck out of the deep, clinging to the rigging of the remaining mast; uppermost, the active figure with the curling hair.

There was a bell on board; and as the ship rolled and dashed, like a desperate creature driven mad, now showing us the whole sweep of her deck, as she turned on her beam-ends towards the shore, now nothing but her keel, as she sprung wildly over and turned towards the sea, the bell rang; and its sound, the knell of those unhappy men,

was borne towards us on the wind. Again we lost her,
and again she rose. Two men were gone. The agony on
shore increased. Men groaned, and clasped their hands;
women shrieked, and turned away their faces. Some ran
wildly up and down along the beach, crying for help
where no help could be. I found myself one of these,
frantically imploring a knot of sailors whom I knew, not
to let those two lost creatures perish before our eyes.

                    Charles Dickens: *David Copperfield.*

(*c*) Time closed up like a fan before him. He saw himself
at one extremity of the years, face to face with the beginning and all the intermediate centuries simultaneously.
Fierce men, clothed in the hides of beasts, and carrying,
for defence and attack, huge clubs and pointed spears,
rose from the rock, like the phantoms before the doomed
Macbeth. They lived in hollows, woods, and mud huts –
perhaps in caves of the neighbouring rocks. Behind them
stood an earlier band. No man was there. Huge elephan-
tine forms, the mastodon, the hippopotamus, the tapir,
antelopes of monstrous size, the megatherium, and the
myledon – all, for the moment, in juxtaposition. Further
back, and overlapped by these, were perched huge-billed
birds and swinish creatures as large as horses. Still more
shadowy were the sinister crocodilian outlines – alligators,
and other uncouth shapes, culminating in the colossal
lizard, the iguanodon. Folded behind were dragon forms
and clouds of flying reptiles: still underneath were fishy
beings of lower development; and so on, till the lifetime
scenes of the fossil confronting him were a present and
modern condition of things.

                    Thomas Hardy: *A Pair of Blue Eyes.*

There is nothing to be said except that in each of these three
passages the novelist's prose has been quickened by the
drama of the situation he has created. It is apt to the
circumstance.

Evidently, then, prose may, under the compulsion of

imaginative thought, have some kinship with poetry. But it is a kinship that makes us a trifle uneasy; we are suspicious of the purple patch, which – I paraphrase the original passage of Horace – he sews on to his normal 'stuff' in order that it may show up brightly at a distance, *late qui splendeat*. Yet when the stuff is able to bear the patch, when they are, in some sort, matched together in texture and colour, the patch is itself amply justified, as in the passages just quoted. There is, however, a kind of prose in which the manner, as it were, takes charge: it is not wrought and fashioned by the urgency or quality of the matter. 'I dare no more write in a fine style', John Wesley is reported to have said, 'than wear a fine coat.' To him the epithet *fine* had a derogatory sense, as indeed it has to us when we speak of 'fine writing'. Hazlitt, shifting the emphasis a little perhaps, called it 'the florid style', which is 'resorted to as a spangled veil to conceal the want of ideas'. 'Flowery' is another epithet we apply to it; and we mean not a style that flowers naturally, of itself, but one that is consciously and artificially ornamental. At its worst it is mere fustian:

> 'Bradman struck the fire of genius out of the match's honest and rather dull rock. The atmosphere became tense and luminous. We could feel that Bradman was the creative force of the day, and while he was at the wicket the hour was enchanted, that in the forge of his batsman-ship molten history was being beaten into shape.' [1]

On its higher levels, it occupies a sort of dim and doubtful no-man's-land between prose and poetry, as often in the work of Walter Pater and John Ruskin, sometimes in Kinglake, sometimes in so fine a writer of ordinary prose as Cardinal Newman. It is, in fact, from Newman that our one example is taken, mainly because its theme is, as it happens, indirectly related to the present argument. The 'he' of the quotation is 'the agent of a London company', and New-

---

[1] Quoted by Sir Donald Bradman in his book *Farewell to Cricket*. It is by Neville Cardus, whom Bradman calls, with implied if not conscious literary criticism, 'the melodramatic Cardus'.

man is describing what this man's prosaic eye would miss as he looked over the Aegean from a height in Attica. An aversion to the agent's prose has betrayed Newman himself into something which is prose aping poetry, a spinning of words and painting of pictures, art for art's sake:

> He would look over the Aegean from the height he had
> ascended; he would follow with his eye the chain of
> islands, which, starting from the Sunian headland,
> seemed to offer the fabled divinities of Attica, when they
> would visit their Ionian cousins, a sort of viaduct thereto
> across the sea: but that fancy would not occur to him, not
> any admiration of the dark violet billows with their white
> edges down below; nor of those graceful, fan-like jets of
> silver upon the rocks, which slowly rise aloft like water
> spirits from the deep, then shiver, and break, and spread,
> and shroud themselves, and disappear, in a soft mist of
> foam; nor of the gentle, incessant heaving and panting
> of the whole liquid plain; nor of the long waves, keeping
> steady time, like a line of soldiery, as they resound upon
> the hollow shore, – he would not deign to notice that
> restless living element at all, except to bless his stars that
> he was not upon it.

3

All that has been said in the previous chapter forces us into some discussion of two very difficult questions – 'What is the difference between prose and poetry?' and 'What is the difference between prose and verse?' The first question is, we may say, concerned with spirit, the second with technical form; but so closely inter-related are form and spirit that this distinction, though it has a certain validity, does not take us very far. Let us approach the subject by way of a familiar passage in Milton:

> Lastly, I should not choose this manner of writing,
> wherein knowing myself inferior to myself, led by the
> genial power of nature to another task, I have the use, as

I may account, but of my left hand. And though I shall be foolish in saying more to this purpose, yet, since it will be such a folly, as wisest men go about to commit, having only confessed and so committed, I may trust with more reason, because with more folly, to have courteous pardon. For although a poet, soaring in the high reason of his fancies, with his garland and singing robes about him, might, without apology, speak more of himself than I mean to do; yet for me sitting here below in the cool element of prose, a mortal thing among many readers of no empyreal conceit, to venture and divulge unusual things of myself, I shall petition to the gentler sort, it may not be envy to me.

It is clear that for Milton poetry and prose are by no means the same thing. Poetry soars, prose remains below. He himself, 'led by the genial power of nature to another task', the task of poetry, has the use 'but of his left hand' at a 'manner of writing' (prose) which is not his choice. 'Below in the cool element of prose' – the implication that prose is prosaic, pedestrian, earth-bound is perfectly plain; yet all the time we catch in this very passage, in the surge of its phrases and its very incoherence, the ascent of poetry – 'soaring in the high reason of his fancies, with his garland and singing robes about him . . .' Still, it is, according to Milton, prose; if it soars, it is only within a range imposed upon it by its form. The garland and the singing robes belong to another medium.

And here we hesitate a little. We are thrown back on to our second question, the difference between prose and verse, out of which arises another: whether verse is the only medium for poetry, as Milton, by implication seems to suggest. Now the difference between the two forms, prose and verse, is a technical one and is within certain limits definable. The underlying element in verse is the recurrence of sound. In early verse this was represented mainly by alliteration occurring systematically in the two halves of a divided line:

swylce self cyning

of bryd-bure,	beah-horda weard,
tryððode tir-fæst	getrume micle,
cystum gecyþed,	ond his cwen mid him
medo- stigge mæt	mægþa hose.

Later, in verse as we usually understand it, it was represented
by the regular fall of the stress – regular rhythm – and often
by echoing sounds usually at the end of the lines – rhyme;
and later still, in much modern verse, by associations of
sound and sense, including repetition, alliteration, assonance, rhyme, and other devices, with a loose general rhythm.
Briefly, there is in verse a certain conscious artifice, or combination of artifices, that gives an effect akin to the 'beat'
of music. Because of this underlying recurrence or regularity,
verse is measured language; it is written, sometimes
obviously, sometimes not, in metrical form. But this is not
true of prose, which is 'straightforward discourse, the
ordinary form of written or spoken language, without
metrical structure' (SOED). There are, then, two forms of
speech and writing, metrical and unmetrical; we have to
inquire how far they may, or may not, be a common
medium for the expression of thought.

The existence of an exalted or 'poetic' prose, whether
naturally arising out of an imaginative or urgent theme or
artificially wrought up as in fine writing, has already been
admitted and exemplified. The question arises whether a
piece of writing in prose form can of itself become a poem;
that is, whether poetry can exist without the sound effects
that belong to verse. There is no absolute answer. It is
arguable that the indefinable something we call poetry can
adapt itself to the separate media, as electricity can be conveyed equally by a wire and an iron rail. But that argument
still leaves something unsaid. We are faced with yet another
question: When something written in prose form is imbued
with imaginative poetic feeling does it still remain prose?
It does if we think of prose as a *form* of writing or speech,

forgetting or ignoring the ambiguity by which the term
prose is used not as the technical opposite of *verse*, but as the
spiritual opposite of *poetry*. This has been made clear in the
note on the Authorized Version of the Bible (p. 179), where
it is suggested that the poems of the Hebrew or Greek are
translated into a form which, though in English it is ostensibly prose, has in fact some of the rhythmical recurrent
elements that belong to the original verse. To put it in more
concrete terms, the famous passage concerning charity in St
Paul's first letter to the Corinthians (xiii) is in English, as it
is in the original Greek, prose; but the song of Moses (Deut.,
xxxii, 1–43) is in English, as it is in the original Hebrew,
poetry.

Let us turn for another example away from the Authorized Version to a very famous passage from an essay by
Walter Pater:

> She is older than the rocks among which she sits; like
> the vampire, she has been dead many times, and learned
> the secrets of the grave; and has been a diver in deep seas,
> and keeps their fallen day about her; and trafficked for
> strange webs with Eastern merchants: and, as Leda, was
> the mother of Helen of Troy, and, as Saint Anne, the
> mother of Mary; and all this has been to her but as the
> sound of lyres and flutes, and lives only in the delicacy
> with which it has moulded the changing lineaments, and
> tinged the eyelids and the hands.

Now it is reasonable to think that Pater himself intended
that to be prose – that is, he wrote it in prose form. It is, in
fact, a piece of rather showy and meretricious fine writing;
but that, for the moment, is neither here nor there. The
interesting thing is that no less a poet than W. B. Yeats saw
in it a metrical poem, and placed it first in the *Oxford Book
of Modern Verse*, arranged as what he called *vers libre*: [1]

> *She is older than the rocks among which she sits;*
> *Like the Vampire,*

She has been dead many times,
And learned the secrets of the grave;
And has been a diver in deep seas,
And keeps their fallen day about her;
And trafficked for strange webs with Eastern merchants;
And, as Leda,
Was the mother of Helen of Troy,
And, as St Anne,
Was the mother of Mary;
And all this has been to her but as the sound of lyres and
*   flutes,*
And lives
Only in the delicacy
With which it has moulded the changing lineaments,
And tinged the eyelids and the hands.

'Pater', says Yeats, 'was accustomed to give each sentence a separate page of manuscript, isolating and analysing its rhythm.' But it is difficult to see how this justifies the reduction of a piece of highly wrought prose to amorphous verse. There is, as modern criticism and practice goes out of its way to emphasize, a real and significant inter-relationship of form and spirit; but it is not evidenced in the chopping up of prose sentences, however florid, into unequal lines; nor is this process, as Yeats seems to suggest, 'of revolutionary importance'.

Sometimes, indeed, prose form and verse meet in a kind of no-man's land – a doubtful, dangerous, and somewhat melancholy place. When the meeting is conscious and deliberate, that is, when the writer merely gives to regularly rhythmical and rhyming lines the fashion of prose, the effect is, in a somewhat trivial way, amusing:

Page and his wife, that made such a strife, we met them twain in Dog Lane; we gave them the wall, and that was all. For Mr Scott, we have seen him not, except as he pass'd, in a wonderful haste, to see a friend in Silver End. Mrs Jones proposes, ere July closes, that she and sister,

and her Jones Mister, and we that are here, our course
shall steer to dine in the Spinney; but for a guinea, if the
weather should hold, so hot and so cold, we had better by
far stay where we are. For the grass there grows, while
nobody mows (which is very wrong), so rank and long,
that so to speak, 'tis at least a week, if it happens to rain,
ere it dries again.

William Cowper: *Letters*.

But when, more seriously, prose develops a regular lilt,
falling loosely into lines that are reminiscent of unrhymed
verse, a form of writing emerges that is neither fish, nor
fowl, nor good red herring. There are instances of this in
the more 'poetic' descriptive flights of Dickens, and it is
common in De Quincey and in Blackmore's *Lorna Doone*:

I had the power, if I could raise myself to will it; and
yet again had not the power, for the weight of twenty
Atlantics was upon me, or the oppression of inexpiable
guilt. 'Deeper than ever plummet sounded,' I lay inactive.
Then like a chorus, the passion deepened. Some greater
interest was at stake, some mightier cause, than ever yet
the sword had pleaded, or trumpet had proclaimed. Then
came sudden alarms; hurryings to and fro; trepidations
of innumerable fugitives, I knew not whether from the
good cause or the bad; darkness and lights; tempest and
human faces; and at last, with the sense that all was lost,
female forms, and the features that were worth all the
world to me; and but a moment allowed – and clasped
hands, with heartbreaking partings, and then – everlasting
farewells! and, with a sigh such as the caves of hell sighed
when the incestuous mother uttered the abhorred name
of Death, the sound was reverberated – everlasting farewells! and again, and yet again reverberated – everlasting
farewells!

And I awoke in struggles, and cried aloud, 'I will sleep
no more!'

Thomas de Quincey: *Confessions of an Opium Eater*.

All above it is strong dark mountain, spread with heath, and desolate, but near our house the valleys cove, and open warmth and shelter. Here are trees, and bright green grass, and orchards full of contentment, and a man may scarce espy the brook, although he hears it everywhere. And indeed a stout good piece of it comes through our farmyard, and swells sometimes to a rush of waves, when the clouds are on the hill-tops. But all below, where the valley bends, and the Lynn stream goes along with it, pretty meadows slope their breast, and the sun spreads on the water. And nearly all of this is ours, till you come to Nicholas Snowe's land.

But about two miles below our farm, the Bagworthy water runs into the Lynn, and makes a real river of it. Thence it hurried away, with strength and a force of wilful waters, under the foot of a bare-faced hill, and so to rocks and woods again, where the stream is covered over, and dark, heavy pools delay it. There are plenty of fish all down this way, and the further you go the bigger they be, having deeper grounds to feed in; and sometimes in the summer months, when mother could spare me off the farm, I came down here, with Annie to help (because it was so lonely), and caught wellnigh a basketful of little trout and minnows, with a hook and a bit of worm on it, or a fern-web, or a blow-fly, hung from a hazel pulse-stick.

R. D. Blackmore: Lorna Doone.

In both passages there are unmistakable droppings (as Silas Wegg would say) into verse, trippings of iambs and anapaests. Certainly, the general effect is not altogether unpleasing. Indeed, no less a critic than George Saintsbury justifies 'this merging and meeting of all sorts of metrical music in the flood of rhythmical prose'. He shows, with approbation, how Ruskin's prose is full of 'blank verses', and sometimes even falls into stanza arrangements, with actual rhyme, like this:

> *And the city lay*
> > *Under its guarding hills*
> > *One labyrinth of delight,*
> > *Its grey and fretted towers*
> > *Misty in their magnificence of* height.[1]

But prose poetry (as distinct from poetic or emotive prose) is, after all, a hybrid, a mongrel form. There is, admittedly, a kind of beauty in it; but it is (though Saintsbury specifically denies this) an illegitimate and 'monstrous' beauty.

However, if there is in much great prose a measure of the poetic, there is also – especially in the light of modern criticism and practice – a place for the prosaic in poetry. Sometimes poetry has a soaring or pictorial or deliberately musical language of its own, allied to and quickened by its expression in the rhythms of verse –

> *That time of year thou mayst in me behold*
> *When yellow leaves, or none, or few, do hang*
> *Upon those boughs which shake against the cold,*
> *Bare ruin'd choirs, where late the sweet birds sang.*

or

> > *Him the Almighty Power*
> *Hurld headlong flaming from th' Ethereal Skie*
> *With hideous ruine and combustion down*
> *To bottomless perdition, there to dwell*
> *In Adamantine Chains and penal Fire,*
> *Who durst defie th' Omnipotent to Arms*

or

> *Perhaps the self-same song that found a path*
> *Through the sad heart of Ruth when, sick for home,*
> > *She stood in tears amid the alien corn;*
> *The same that ofttimes hath*
> *Charm'd magic casements opening on the foam*
> *Of perilous seas, in faery lands forlorn.*

Those passages illustrate the common man's commonest notion of poetry. And it is a sound notion. We recognize the

[1] *A History of English Prose Rhythm.*

poet most easily when he has his singing robes about him. But, as Wordsworth pointed out in the Preface to *Lyrical Ballads*, the language of poetry is not a thing reserved, invariable, apart. His famous manifesto has been often quoted, but its opening declaration is worth quoting again:

> 'The principal object, then, proposed in these poems was to choose incidents and situations from common life, and to relate or describe them, throughout, as far as was possible in a selection of language really used by men, and, at the same time to throw over them a certain colouring of imagination, whereby ordinary things should be presented to the mind in an unusual aspect.'

He is saying, in effect, that the poetry is not primarily (though it is partly) in the language, but in that 'colouring of imagination' that is thrown over it, and restating the principle of the correspondence of matter and manner – common life is related in common language. Though he has in mind some of the artificial 'poetic diction' of his own and a previous age, he recognizes, in a previous paragraph, that expression in poetry 'must in different eras have excited very different expectations'. His general argument has been taken further and modified by many modern critics, notably Mr T. S. Eliot, who says that though 'no poetry is ever exactly the same speech that the poet talks and hears', it 'has to be in such a relation to the speech of his time that the listener or reader can say "that is how I should talk if I could talk poetry"', and asserts that 'the music of poetry must be a music latent in the common speech of the time'.

But however persuasively this argument, for the 'prosaic' in poetry, has been put by modern critics and exemplified in the work of modern practitioners there remains for most of us, even when we are prepared and willing to depart from a purely traditional view, a lurking doubt of its validity. The reviewer of Mr Eliot's own *Prufrock* in *The Times Literary Supplement* some forty years ago said that the things which occurred to the mind of Mr Eliot . . . certainly have no relation to "poetry" ', and declared that he gave an example only because, on the word of Mr Eliot himself, they had appeared 'in a periodical which claims that word as its title'. Poor man! he had no eye for a poetic revolution; but deep down in what we now consider his blundering criticism there is an element of truth.

It is fashionable now to vindicate and admire Wordsworth's more extreme experiments, to find hidden depths of poetry in, for example,

> *'Few months of life has he in store,*
> *As he to you will tell,*
> *For still the more he works, the more*
> *His poor old ancles swell'*

and

> *'You see a little muddy pond*
> *Of water, never dry;*
> *I've measured it from side to side*
> *'Tis three feet long, and two feet wide.'*

But it is worth while, as a corrective, turning to the section in Coleridge's *Biographia Literaria* in which he examines the 'tenets peculiar to Mr Wordsworth' and the whole theory of metrical language:

'The true question', he says, 'must be, whether there are not modes of expression, a construction, and an order of sentences, which are in their fit and natural place in a serious prose composition, but would be disproportionate and heterogeneous in metrical poetry; and, *vice versa*, whether in the language of a serious poem there may not be an arrangement both of words and sentences, and a use and selection of (what are called) figures of speech, both as to their kind, their frequency, and their occasions, which on a subject of equal weight would be vicious and alien in correct and manly prose.'

Meanwhile, it is worth while keeping in mind a truth, or an idea, advanced by Mr Eliot himself that 'in a poem of any

length, there must be transitions between passages of greater
and less intensity, to give a rhythm of fluctuating emotion
essential to the musical structure of the whole; and the
passages of less intensity will be, in relation to the level on
which the whole poem operates, prosaic'. This is, in a sense,
only a restatement of Wordsworth's principle, that there
must be thrown over the whole thing 'a certain colouring of
imagination', and that the theme must be 'presented to the
mind in an unusual aspect'. When, for example, we read
(in *The Waste Land*) this passage:

> *Well, if Albert won't leave you alone, there it is, I said,*
> *What you get married for if you don't want children?*
> HURRY UP PLEASE IT'S TIME
> *Well, that Sunday Albert was home, they had a hot gam-*
>   *mon,*
> *And they asked me in to dinner, to get the beauty of it hot*
> HURRY UP PLEASE IT'S TIME
> HURRY UP PLEASE IT'S TIME
> *Goonight Bill. Goonight Lou. Goonight May. Goonight*
> *Ta ta. Goonight, Goonight.*
> *Good night, ladies, good night, sweet ladies, good*
> *night, good night.*

We are not justified in isolating it and treating it by itself;
its deliberate (and mannered) colloquialism is a reflection
of the 'fluctuating emotion' of the poem as a whole. A
simpler example will make the point clearer. Here is the
first stanza of a familiar poem by Henry Reed:

> *To-day we have naming of parts. Yesterday*
> *We had daily cleaning. And to-morrow morning,*
> *We shall have what to do after firing. But to-day,*
> *To-day we have naming of parts. Japonica*
> *Glistens like coral in all of the neighbouring gardens,*
>   *And to-day we have naming of parts.*

Now in that, and in each of the four succeeding stanzas, the
contrast of 'prosaic' (the formalized military jargon of the
NCO) and the 'poetic' ('Japonica Glistens like coral . . .')

deliberately points the theme of contrast – the ordinary commonplace lesson on the rifle set against the background of the immutable, indifferent, and beautiful natural world. The poetry is in the whole.

Even so, certain problems arise. We have to decide from the reading of the whole poem whether, in fact, the 'fluctuating emotion' or the 'colouring of imagination' is, in fact, there to sustain the language. Here is a short extract from a review [1] of Mr William Plomer's collection of light satirical poems, *A Shot in the Park*:

'The charm of Mr Plomer's verse resides, in fact, in his hesitant sympathy with his subjects, the restraint of his strokes, the ambiguity of his aim:

> *On the back of his motor-bike*
> *They're off to the Crala Hop,*
> *She'll wear her apricot nylon dress,*
> *Her shoes from the Co-op.*'

It is difficult for the reader who, like myself, has not read the whole poem, to see in those four lines hesitant sympathy, ambiguity of aim, or even restraint of stroke; difficult, for that matter, to understand why, if they do exist, these qualities constitute 'the charm of Mr Plomer's verse'. For, not to put too fine a point upon it, this quatrain, isolated as it is by the reviewer, is plain doggerel. True, in its setting, as part of a whole poem, it may be 'prosaic' only in the relative sense. But the tendency of modern criticism to read into the colloquial profundities and significances that are not really there, to imagine that it has some odd inverted poetic quality of its own, is one that the common reader should resist. Not that doggerel is always colloquial; it may be 'poetic'. It arises when a trivial thought is expressed in verse, or when a worthy or even imaginative thought is versified in language unworthy of it; when (in verse, for doggerel is not associated with prose form) manner and matter do not correspond. In the theorists of

[1] *The Times Literary Supplement*, April 29, 1955.

the colloquial – Wordsworth himself and many modern
poet-critics – the 'prosaic' often becomes fatuous; in the
theorists of the 'poetic', the language, like Macbeth's
ambition, 'o'er leaps itself, and falls on the other' – as it
does often in Keats, a poet who was more justly assessed by
contemporary critics than we sometimes care to admit.

Matter and manner – we cannot escape them. When they
are at one, when what is said has a perfect correspondence
with the way of saying it, we have good writing (or speech)
on any level. But when this law of appropriateness is broken,
writing (or speech) becomes in varying degrees bad. And
here, with reference to literature – the highest level of
writing – an interesting question arises, whether, after all,
these distinctions of prose and poetry and prose and verse
are real, or merely literary conventions. On this Mr J.
Middleton Murry has something to say in his book *The
Problem of Style* (Lecture iii). In the end he has to leave the
question unanswered, merely advancing and elaborating the
argument that prose may be 'prosaic' or 'poetic', and that
certain verse may have the characteristics of prose. Since his
book was published (1922) great developments have taken
place in English literary expression, especially in verse. Any
answer (if there is one) to the question must be related to
the principles that underlie the technique and form of verse
writing, especially in the light of theory and practice today.
They are briefly outlined in the next chapter.

4

With the question of the general relationship of poetry
and prose is bound up another – Has the prose of the poet
any special characteristics that derive from his practice of
poetry? It is a question that is discussed in a famous essay
by Hazlitt, *The Prose Style of the Poets*, which begins
with the uncompromising sentence, 'I have but an indifferent opinion of the prose-style of poets: not that it is
not sometimes good, nay, excellent; but it is never the
better, and generally the worse, from the habit of writing

verse'. Hazlitt's main argument seems to be two-fold: first, that the poet is fanciful, immersed 'in sensual ideas', 'craving after continual excitements', while the prose-writer, having 'a remote practical purpose', is condemned to a 'severity of composition' that 'damps the enthusiasm'; second, that the poet is accustomed to a syntactical freedom, in which 'a greater number of inversions, or a latitude in the transposition of words is allowed, which is not conformable to the strict laws of prose'. The argument seems, and indeed is, peculiarly naïve. Between two outward forms of writing, prose and poetry, Hazlitt assumes an imaginative or 'spiritual' difference that can be almost mathematically defined; and he unduly emphasizes the importance of certain syntactical differences that distinguish verse from prose form. He does not, in fact, escape the confusions which always threaten when we use the terms prose, verse, and poetry.

Nevertheless, it is profitable to follow Hazlitt a little further. He ends the essay with the statement: 'Milton's prose-style savours too much of poetry, and . . . of an imitation of Latin. Dryden's is perfectly unexceptionable, and a model, in simplicity, strength, and perspicuity, for the subjects he treats of.' There is no suggestion here, and Hazlitt does not appear to realize, that Milton was writing before what he himself called a 'familiar style' had been hammered out in English. Indeed, he praises, somewhat paradoxically, the style of the older writers who were not poets (like Jeremy Taylor) because it was *poetical* in the favourable sense; and indulges in a long digression on Burke's prose because the principle underlying it is 'truth, not beauty – not pleasure, but power'. In other words, he appears in one part of the essay to rate high that very sublimity which in another essay (*On Familiar Style*) he denies to prose.

Of the relationship of Dryden's prose to his poetry he says nothing. It is arguable, however, that the discipline of the heroic couplet, with its epigrammatic succinctness and its colloquial (if stylized) language, is reflected in the prose of Dryden; though there is no evidence that the syntactical pattern of heroic verse, with its inversions, ellipses, and the like, affected the construction of his prose sentences. Here, indeed, we are on difficult and doubtful ground. Hazlitt advances the fanciful theory that 'Dr Johnson endeavoured to give an air of dignity and novelty to his diction by affecting the order of words usual in poetry'. That is, among other things, to imply that Johnson was primarily a poet. But the proposition is not demonstrably true. The syntactical order of words in Johnsonian prose is not, in fact, noticeably different from the normal order; and neither his Latinized vocabulary nor his addiction to antithesis, the chief characteristic of his prose style, can properly, or at any rate convincingly, be related to his style in verse. Similarly, of Pope, Hazlitt says that 'his prose is timid and constrained, and his verse inclining to the monotonous'. The criticism of the prose is in a measure just; but Hazlitt has no conception of the amazing adjustment of syntax to rhythm by which Pope avoids that very monotony of which he speaks.

Strangely enough, Hazlitt does not mention Gray, except in a passing reference. But Gray is a remarkable example of a poet whose style in prose and style in verse stand very much apart. Though in his poetic themes he leant towards the 'romantic', his poetic diction is in the highly formalized tradition of the eighteenth century. But he is often acclaimed one of the greatest of English letter writers because his prose is syntactically simple, often colloquial, easy, and informal:

As to Cambridge it is, as it was, for all the World; & the People are, as they were; & Mr Trollope is as he was, that is, half ill, half well. I wish with all my Heart they were all better, but what can one do? there is no News, only I think I heard a Whisper, as if the Vice-Chancellour should be with Child (but I beg you not to mention this, for I may come into trouble about it); there is some Suspicion, that the Professor of Mathematicks had a

Hand in the thing. Dr Dickens says the University will be obliged to keep it, as it was got, in Magistratu.

I was going to tell you how sorry I am for your Illness, but, I hope, it is too late to be sorry now: I can only say, that I really *was* very sorry. may you live a hundred Christmases, & eat as many Collars of brawn stuck with Rosemary. Adieu, I am sincerely Yours T G:

Gray was not so much a poet fallen, as Matthew Arnold alleged, on an age of prose, as a writer who naturally maintained a difference between prose and poetry. When he put on his singing robes he resorted to a singing idiom. So, too, Cowper, whom Hazlitt also ignores; but not to the same degree. Cowper's letters, less colloquial and in certain ways less informal, than Gray's are written in an easy flowing prose that suggests cultured speech. To them may be applied the phrase which Coleridge, thinking rather of theme than style, uses of *The Task* – 'divine chit-chat'. But his poetic language has its own formalities, and slips frequently into a conventional diction that befits his simple metrical patterns. Still, the prose is to be traced in the poetry, and the poetry in the prose:

> *Now stir the fire, and close the shutters fast,*
> *Let fall the curtains, wheel the sofa round,*
> *And, while the bubbling and loud hissing urn*
> *Throws up a steamy column, and the cups,*
> *That cheer but not inebriate, wait on each,*
> *So let us welcome peaceful evening in.*

In that familiar passage are the two Cowpers; the first two lines, although in the metrical rhythm of verse, have the flow of his prose, but the 'hissing urn', the 'steamy column', and the balanced phrase 'cheer but not inebriate' belong to his poetry. Nevertheless, between the prose of the letters and the blank verse of *The Task* there is by no means the difference that lies between Gray's intimate prose style and, say, *The Bard* or even the *Elegy*.

It is significant that the two poets whom Hazlitt praises

most highly for their prose are 'the poet laureate' (Southey) and 'the Author of *Rimini*, and Editor of the *Examiner*' (Leigh Hunt); significant because Hazlitt, writing as a contemporary, does not seem to realize what has become a truism of later criticism, that both Southey and Hunt were prose-writers first, and poets afterwards. That, in a sense, is true of Cowper also; but whereas his prose has a kinship with his poetry, the turgidities of most of Southey's and Leigh Hunt's verse have little relationship to their prose – Southey's (says Hazlitt justly) 'with nothing awkward, circuitous, or feeble in it', Hunt's, which has the 'tone of lively, sensible conversation'. But Hazlitt more than stretches a point when he says that Hunt's prose has 'the raciness, the sharpness, and sparkling effect of poetry', or implies that its almost trivial lightness betokens the fact that 'he had escaped the shackles of rhyme'. So, too, he goes astray when he says, 'I should almost guess the Author of *Waverley* to be a writer of ambling verses from the desultory vacillation and want of firmness in the march of his style'. Scott may have written 'ambling verses' – though the word is not quite apt or even just – and his prose has (except in his admirable use of colloquial dialect) a rotundity of expression linked with certain weaknesses of construction and syntax. But to attribute this to the fact that he was first (chronologically speaking) a verse writer is to imagine a relationship where no relationship exists.

The only poet who is a poet first and a prose-writer afterwards with whom Hazlitt deals at all seriously is Coleridge. But he makes no real attempt to show any relationship of the prose to the poetry. Coleridge, he says, 'an incessant craving, as it were, to exalt every idea into a metaphor, to expand every sentiment into a lengthened mystery, voluminous and vast, confused and cloudy. His style is not succinct, but incumbered with a train of words and images that have no practical, and only a possible relation to one another – that add to its stateliness, but impede its march'. That is no more than to say that frequently in his prose Coleridge expresses tortuous philosophical thought in a kind of language appropriate to it – the Mr Skionar of Peacock, 'a transcendental poet', from '*skias onar*, umbriae somnium'. But the texture of Coleridge's prose is not noticeably 'confused and cloudy' when he is treating of a specific subject – in, for example, the chapters in *Biographia Literaria* on the tenets of Wordsworth. True, it is not in the 'familiar style'; it is a learned prose couched in a formalized literary language:

> As little can I agree with the assertion, that from the objects with which the rustic hourly communicates the best part of language is formed. For first, if to communicate with an object implies such an acquaintance with it, as renders it capable of being discriminately reflected on, the distinct knowledge of an uneducated rustic would furnish a very scanty vocabulary. The few things and modes of action requisite for his bodily conveniences would alone be individualized; while all the rest of nature would be expressed by a small number of confused general terms.

But it is difficult to trace any connexion between this prose and the verse of Coleridge's finest poetry – *The Ancient Mariner*, *Kubla Khan*, *Christabel*, and, say, *Frost at Midnight*. In that Coleridge was a poet of unusual imagination and an unusual command of poetic imagery, it is reasonable to suppose that sometimes an excess of imagery 'incumbered' his prose style. But that is as far as we can go. The pattern of the prose and the pattern of the poetry are different. It is only in the semi-poetical prose marginal gloss to *The Ancient Mariner* that there is an obvious link between Coleridge the prose-writer and Coleridge the poet.

To do Hazlitt justice, however, he makes no serious attempt to trace any prose-verse connexion especially on syntactical grounds; though in a vague and confused way (as, for example, in his ambiguous use of the term 'poetical prose') he implies it. That there should be some common element in the poetry and prose of a writer who excels, though it may be not equally, in both is scarcely to be denied;

but the difference, syntactical, idiomatic, and rhythmical, between the two media (assuming verse to be the usual medium of poetry) is such that detailed and analytical comparison is almost, if not quite, invalidated. That is especially true when the prose concerned is expository. Hazlitt, rather strangely, does not mention Wordsworth; but his prose style in the famous Preface to the *Lyrical Ballads* and his verse style in many of the poems themselves together make a curious commentary on his pronouncement that the language of poetry did not fundamentally differ from the language of prose. There are examples after Hazlitt's time. It might be possible, for example, to find some common element in the prose and poetry of Arnold – a certain limpidity, perhaps, a certain quality of diction; but it would be difficult to relate the syntactical and idiomatic pattern of T. S. Eliot's poetry with the prose of his criticism. All that can be said (and that hesitantly) is that sometimes he submits a trifle reluctantly to the discipline of the prose sentence.

The case is, perhaps, a little different with the poets who were also imaginative prose-writers – that is, novelists. Straining a point a little, and being wise, as it were, after the event, we could find in a poem of Emily Brontë's – 'No coward soul is mine', for example – a kind of crystallized version of the prose of *Wuthering Heights*. The relationship of Meredith's prose to his poetry is more complicated; something of its idiosyncrasies remain in the poems, but they are subordinated to the demands of fine metrical experiment and effect.

In prose Meredith was often diffuse, involved, wasteful of words and images. His poetry points forward to the modern manner, in which words and images are semantically and symbolically highly charged. 'Unessentials,' says W. T. Young in *The Cambridge History of English Literature*, 'are shorn away until words are left to stand side by side, each preserving, sphinx-like, the secret which connects it with other words.' In Meredith the two media brought out different qualities, though it is possible to argue that they were in some sense complementary. There is here some kind

of parallel with Hardy. Poetry was Hardy's first love, and
he too points forward to the modern manner. His words,
sometimes incongruously classical, sometimes almost
ostentatiously native, are packed together with a fine dis-
regard for conventional music, but except in his rather
frequent less inspired moments, strangely evocative and
(like Meredith's) highly charged. Some of the incongruities
of language and something of the carelessness of diction are
apparent in the prose of the novels, where they fail of their
effect. But it is curious that in his finest descriptive passages
of prose, which have, in the best sense, a 'poetic' quality,
the style is not in any way crabbed or awkward. His sentences rise and fall with a beautiful rhythm that always
remains, however, the authentic rhythm of prose, not the
bastard rhythm of verse. It is interesting to imagine how
Hardy would have recast as a poem the passage (in *Far From
the Madding Crowd*) where he describes the landscape and
the skyscape as seen from Norcombe Hill, when 'the roll of
the world eastward is almost a palpable movement', or that
other passage (in *A Pair of Blue Eyes*) where Knight sees
'Time close up as a fan before him' as he clings desperately
to Cliff without a Name.

Interesting – but perhaps not altogether profitable. We
cannot escape the conception of the 'poet with his singing
robe about him' and the 'writer moving in the cool regions
of prose'. The ultimate difference between prose and poetry
remains, as we have already reminded ourselves, something
of an enigma; and even in a single writer the relationship
between the two cannot easily or with any confidence be
defined.

5

But a rather curious question remains: Is it possible for
literature to be written in a 'bad' style? In answering, or
attempting to answer, it we will confine ourselves to prose.
At the outset, we are faced with a kind of contradiction in
terms, or at any rate a problem of definition. If we accept
the doctrine, that in good writing there must be a corre-

spondence between matter and manner, we imply that the
style which arises out of this correspondence is itself good –
or, leaving out epithets altogether, that such writing has
style. True, this correspondence can exist on a lower level –
as (I hope) in the writing of this book. But on this level we
will (in order to clear the decks) dispense with the word
'style' altogether, speaking rather of 'English apt to the
subject'. To return then, to literature. I shall take as a
starting-point a statement of Mr Eliot concerning Thomas
Hardy: 'He was indifferent even to the prescripts of good
writing: he wrote sometimes overpowering well, but always
carelessly; at times his style touches sublimity without ever
having passed through the stage of being good.' In that
sentence there are certain implications which deserve comment and suggest a way of tackling the question we have
asked ourselves.

It is necessary at the outset to inquire what Mr Eliot
means by 'the prescripts of good writing'. In view of what
follows, these prescripts seem to be nothing more, or less,
than the principles of usage – almost, pressing the point a
little, the principles of grammar. The old problem of the
great writer's freedom from a defiance of the commonly
accepted laws of 'good' English, as enunciated by, for
example, Fowler and Partridge, crops up again. A friend of
mine once confessed that he could never read the Wessex
novels with perfect pleasure because Hardy was given to
splitting infinitives. It would be stretching a point to assume
that Mr Eliot had in mind such a venial sin as this. But he
was, no doubt, thinking of Hardy's lapses in the actual
construction of his sentences – such loose relationships, for
example, as these:

> Like all people who have known rough times, light-
> heartedness seemed to her too irrational and inconsequent
> to be indulged in as a reckless dram now and then.

And

> On reaching the hill the sun had quite disappeared.

But they are not very frequent, and in any case they are such as occur in the writing of most recognized novelists – in Charlotte Brontë, in Dickens, in Wells, in Arnold Bennett. 'No one bothers to write grammatically now' – thus the Critics, and they were right for the past as well as for the present. There are times when, as far as grammar is concerned, the great writer is all astray, and pedantry cannot say a word; still less, now that syntax itself is, or seems to be, in the melting pot.

The indictment of carelessness is different only in degree. 'Hardy,' says Mr Eliot, 'sometimes writes supremely well, and always carelessly.' Apparently, then, excellence of writing and carelessness are not incompatible qualities. But 'carelessness' also requires a little definition. In Hardy it is, in the main, a kind of stiltedness which betrays him into complicated ungainly sentences of this kind:

> She did not divine the ample explanation of his manner, without personal vanity, that was afforded by the fact of Donald being the depository of Henchard's confidence in respect of his past treatment of the pale, chastened mother who walked by her side.

And

> The pain she experienced from the almost absolute obliviousness to her existence that was shown by the pair of them because at times half dissipated by her sense of its humorousness.

It is almost as if, not having an academic University background, he feels that in some way he must be academic; he writes consciously like a schoolboy who feels that his sentences are all the better for a few convolutions; and uses Latin turns of expression when simpler ones are possible and more appropriate, as when he writes 'the remote celestial phenomenon had been pressed into sublunary service as a lover's signal'. This kind of paradoxical careful carelessness is peculiar to Hardy. But equally to other writers there are other types of carelessness; for carelessness itself after all, may be nothing more than an idiosyncrasy of style, prose as distinct from poetic licence. There, indeed, lies the explanation of Mr Eliot's final rather obscure paradox, that Hardy's style 'touches sublimity without ever having passed through the stage of being good'. This is only to say what Mr Eliot himself said (see pp. 196–7), that we judge literature as a whole and not in part. Homer sometimes nods, but he wrote the *Iliad*; Hardy is sometimes ungrammatical, always (according to Mr Eliot) careless, but he wrote *The Mayor of Casterbridge*.

In *Early Victorian Novelists* Lord David Cecil devotes a paragraph to enumerating the defects of Charlotte Brontë's style, its slovenliness, its turbidity, its insensibility 'to the quality and capacity of language', its undisciplined rhetoric. But his next paragraph begins like this:

> 'All the same, Charlotte Brontë's writing is a powerful agent in her effect. For she manages to infuse her personality into it. Cliché, rhetoric and bad grammar alike are pulsing with her intensity, fresh with her charm. Moreover, her strange imagination expresses itself in her actual choice of words. There is hardly a page where we do not meet, sandwiched between commonplace and absurdity, some evocative image, some haunting, throbbing cadence.'

This is to say that there is something in the style of a great writer which transcends what technical defects it may have; the whole is greater than the sum of its parts. 'The intricate question of method in fiction,' says Mr E. M. Forster (*Aspects of the Novel*), 'resolves itself into the power of the writer to bounce the reader into accepting what he says.' If he can do that, other elements, such as grammar and syntax, can (he implies) take care of themselves.[1]

The paradox that underlies the relationship of 'mechanics' is always present and has always been recognized. It is

[1] Certain suggestions in this paragraph, including the quotation from E. M. Forster, are vaguely remembered from a wireless talk the name of whose author I have, alas! forgotten.

there not only in literature but in every art – in, we might say, every activity of man, however ordinary and commonplace. George Herbert, in his quaint fashion, gives it a religious meaning in a little poem which he calls, significantly, 'The Elixer' –

> '*Who sweeps a room, as for thy laws,*
> *Makes that and th' action fine*'.

Browning sees it in the realm of art. Andrea del Sarto is 'called the faultless painter'; but Raphael, 'reaching above and through his art' has that indefinable excellence to which he can never attain:

> '*That arm is wrongly put – and there again –*
> *A fault to pardon in the drawing's lines,*
> *Its body, so to speak: its soul is right,*
> *He means right – that, a child may understand.*
> *Still, what an arm! and I could alter it:*
> *But all the play, the insight and the stretch –*
> *Out of me, out of me!*'

and even Tennyson, himself the perfect craftsman, recognizes it in physical beauty:

> '*. . . a cold and clear-cut face, as I found when her carriage*
> *past,*
> *Perfectly beautiful: let it be granted her: where is the fault?*
> *All that I saw (for her eyes were downcast, not to be seen)*
> *Faultily faultless, icily regular, splendidly null,*
> *Dead perfection, no more.*'

It is only by such an oxymoron as 'the imperfection of perfection' that we can suggest an inward quality which is beyond our defining.

POSTSCRIPT

THE Reading Room of the British Museum is a fine and private place. True, we who go there from time to time are in the midst of company. Men and women walk noiselessly about, or sit studious and intent, the books arrayed before them, the pens or pencils moving silently over the paper. But each is dwelling by himself, alone, in some little corner, or exploring the unknown and half-known territories of the vast world of words. The almost imperceptible rustling of pages breaks the silence of that domed and circular arena of the literature of wasted time. I never pass out of this quiet haunt of bookworms into the bustle of the streets of Bloomsbury without a sense of wonder. The bus driver, the man selling evening papers near the corner of Museum Street, the woman behind the coffee urn at the Express Dairy where I get my morning snack – have they any notion of the activities of that industrious literary beehive a stone's throw away from them? What's —— to them, or they to ——? The name of any author will fit the blank, though it may not satisfy the rhythm. Out here, the catalogues, the innumerable tomes, the products of printing-houses and publishers seem not a few yards but innumerable miles away. I have strayed out of Time past into the Time present of a different and real and pulsing world.

A sense of wonder, but also a suspicion of which I am secretly a little ashamed. It is commonly held that one of the chief enrichments of life is reading. 'Reading,' says Bacon, 'maketh a full man.' But then Bacon was thinking of scholars, not of Tom, Dick, and Harry, or of Bottom, Quince, and Snug, who confessed he was 'hard of study'. True, during the past hundred years or so, we have tried to make scholars of Tom, Dick, and Harry; or, at any rate, to guide and encourage them in the art or mystery of good reading, to introduce them (as the schoolmasters and editors have it) to their great heritage of English literature. Eng. Lit.

has its proud place in the school time-table. Every year, about September, thousands of fifth-formers begin on their painful progress through a little batch of 'set books' selected from the English classics, drawing steadily nearer and nearer to the awful climax of the next midsummer, when, like Portia and Nerissa, they are 'charged upon inter'gatories', and are required to 'answer all things faithfully'. 'They will read me in schools,' growled Tennyson when he felt tolerably certain of his continuing fame, 'and they will call me that horrible Tennyson.' There is a wealth of truth in the saying, and a moral of which the educationists are slow to take heed.

And so I approach, hesitantly and with some reluctance, my personal confession. It is briefly this, that reading (of literature) is not so important as we like to pretend it is. It is, of course, arguable that my life is less rich than it might be if I do not read good books, because I am missing something which is available to all. That is true of everything. My life is equally less rich if I do not play chess, or collect postage-stamps, or spend my evenings watching television. In this matter there are no absolutes. It would be hard to maintain that a man who gives his nights and days to Shakespeare (or Addison, as Johnson recommended) leads a richer life than the man who spends his leisure in playing golf. Every man hath business and desire such as it is. The trouble is that because reading is a necessary or, at any rate, desirable 'skill' in the modern world, we tend to imagine that reading in another sense – that is, the perusal and study of books, preferably 'classical' – is a kind of fundamental. We do not assume the same of any other cultural art, if the phrase will serve. 'I have no ear,' said Charles Lamb, '. . . you will understand me to say – for *music*.' He was only faintly and (in his usual manner) whimsically apologetic about it. All his life, he said, he had been practising 'God save the King' and had not yet 'arrived within many quavers of it'. The simple fact was that music was beyond him. So it is, as it happens, with me. If every cornet, flute, harp, sackbut, psaltery, dulcimer, and all kinds of musick were banished from the earth tomorrow, I should not care a jot. But how Lamb and I differ, in essence, from the man who confesses that he would not care if every piece of literature ever written were burnt up in one vast bonfire I find it a little difficult to understand.

And yet – In his famous invocation to Urania, the Muse of divine inspiration, Milton calls upon her to find 'fit audience, though few' for his lofty song. It is a tacit admission that the reading, no less than the writing, of literature is an art only to be achieved by a certain discipline of the mind and a cultivation of the imaginative faculty. I used the term 'every piece of literature' advisedly in the last sentence of the previous paragraph; 'every book' would have been too sweeping. Since early days of compulsory education, most men read something. Even the golfing addict sneaks home after a poor round and spends an hour or so at his *Golf Made Easy*. Today, in spite of the counter attractions of the cinema, the wireless, and television, which tend to draw us away from the printed page by a direct appeal to the eye and the ear, reading still triumphantly holds its own. But most of it, both light and serious, is on a level that falls below the level of literature. The bookshops are full of books that either lightly entertain or satisfy an insistent and healthy demand for factual knowledge. Whether such reading helps in encouraging and stimulating an appreciation of literature itself is, perhaps, open to doubt. On the whole, I think it does. It has been the general argument of this book that such appreciation can be truly intelligent and satisfying only if the reader recognizes the fact that one important element in literature is the technique of its language, its syntactical idiom. The importance of this is obvious if the 'general' reader (not yet accustomed to the higher flights) is to appreciate, or even understand, some modern prose and much modern poetry. Certainly there is today a keen and welcome interest in 'grammar' and points of usage; but it is largely concerned with the bread-and-butter English we all have to use, as I am trying to use it now, and read professionally or in our ordinary quest for knowledge. I have tried to show in these pages that there is, on the highest level, another English; related to that we are accustomed to in our ordinary reading but in certain respects differing from it; and that this must be taken into account if we are to cultivate reading as an art.

So, in a sense I have to unsay something of what I said, a trifle recklessly, in the opening paragraphs of this Post-script. After all, for the very reason that English is our native language, we all have a start, as it were, over the man who 'has no music in himself' but aspires to understand and appreciate music. Not being willing to cast every book into the bonfire, we leave ourselves a kind of bridge to the books that belong to literature. Language is a common heritage, and in proportion as we understand it at all its levels, literature becomes a common heritage also. The audience must still be fit, but it need not always be few. There are, indeed, signs that it is growing today, though it must be admitted that the 'literary' writers and critics are not as helpful, in this very matter of syntax, as they might be. I have said that the reading of literature is a discipline. So it is; but even a discipline is not to be abused. It must not be allowed to destroy the pleasure that is also at the heart of reading. The trouble is that the man who writes in a private idiom gives pleasure only to a private audience; others who for various reasons feel that his work is worthy of being read, discover in it only a literary puzzle that is very difficult to solve. Obscurity in modern imaginative literature, prose as well as poetry, is not a mere myth. It is a very real thing; and much of it arises, as has already been hinted in this book, from syntactical and idiomatic experiment. I often listen, with interest, to the Critics on the wireless. When they have to deal with a book in 'modernist' idiom, especially a volume of poems, there is usually one among them who candidly confesses that he cannot understand it, because the language itself, its very texture, is a barrier. That candid critic stands for the common man – the man, I mean, who has disciplined himself in the pleasure of reading what I will call 'conventional literature'. When we have made all allowance for the general impression, for the total effect, for the imagination so powerful that it cannot find expression in the ordinary range and order of words, it seems reasonable to expect that literature should have some recognizable relation to the conventions of the language in which it is expressed. At any rate, so it seems to me.

'In 1757,' wrote Dr Johnson, 'Gray published *The Progress of Poesy* and *The Bard*, two compositions at which the readers of poetry were at first content to gaze in mute amazement. Some that tried them confessed their inability to understand them, though Warburton said that they were understood as well as the works of Milton and Shakespeare, which it is the fashion to admire. Garrick wrote a few lines in their praise. Some hardy champions undertook to rescue them from neglect, and in a short time many were content to be shown beauties they could not see.' A few paragraphs later he made his own confession. 'I am,' he wrote, 'one of those that are willing to be pleased, and therefore would gladly find the meaning of the first stanza of *The Progress of Poesy*.' 'Gladly find the meaning' – such an apparently reasonable ambition is now out of fashion. Understanding in the Johnsonian sense is not a necessary step to appreciation. A century later Tennyson was having trouble with Browning. He said of *Sordello* that he could understand only two lines of it, the first ('Who will shall hear Sordello's story told') and the last ('Who would has heard Sordello's story told'), and they were both lies. But of Browning's poetry in general he wrote: 'As for his obscurity in his great imaginative analyses, I believe it is a mistake to explain poetry too much, people have really a pleasure in discovering their own interpretations.' That is in the modern mood, though probably by 'their own interpretations', Tennyson did not mean precisely what is meant by modern poets and critics. He would have more than a little sympathy with Johnson's desire to get at the meaning. Interpretation itself must have something to go upon.

But today understanding and interpretation are unnaturally divorced. The reasonable discipline of the reader is too often defeated by the indiscipline of the poet and, to a less extent, the prose-writer. In that way, modernist literature has become a cult, in which, though for different reasons, many, as Johnson said, are content to be shown beauties which they cannot see. Of this the indiscriminate and lavish praise given to Dylan Thomas's incantation *Under Milk Wood* is a good modern example. When for technical reasons, reasons of syntax and idiom, literature becomes a kind of carefully guarded preserve, both language and literature are apt to suffer. I cannot do better than end by turning again to Somerset Maugham. He is not, it is true, writing of modernist literature, but the application may be easily and justly made:

> Some writers who do not think clearly are inclined to suppose that their thoughts have a significance greater than at first sight appears. It is flattering to believe that they are too profound to be expressed so clearly that all who run may read, and very naturally it does not occur to such writers that the fault is with their own minds which have not the faculty of precise reflection. Here again the magic of the written word obtains. It is very easy to persuade oneself that a phrase that one does not quite understand may mean a great deal more than one realizes. From this there is only a little way to go to fall into the habit of setting down one's impressions in all their original vagueness. Fools can always be found to discover a hidden sense in them. There is another form of wilful obscurity that masquerades as aristocratic exclusiveness. The author wraps his meaning in mystery so that the vulgar shall not participate in it. His soul is a secret garden into which the elect may penetrate only after overcoming a number of perilous obstacles. But this kind of obscurity is not only pretentious; it is shortsighted. For time plays it an odd trick. If the sense is meagre time reduces it to a meaningless verbiage that no one thinks of reading.

Hard words: but they have a moral for today.

BOOKS FOR FURTHER READING

IN the preceding pages I have mentioned a number of books applicable to this or that particular aspect of the subject. Unless an adverse comment has been made, it may be assumed that these books are warmly recommended; I shall not repeat them here.

There were, however, several very good books insufficiently described or indicated, and a few general books not mentioned at all.

I have presupposed a certain elementary knowledge of English literature and language. Such knowledge can be either refurbished or salutarily amplified by an attentive reading of the following works:

LITERATURE

D. M. Davin and John Mulgan, *An Introduction to English Literature* (Oxford University Press), modern, alert, 'human', readable, yet dependable and academically sound.

LANGUAGE

Simeon Potter, *Our Language* (Penguin Books), a very attractive presentation by a true scholar – and, to complement it, that excellent, although far more formal book, *The English Language*, by C. L. Wrenn; shorter than either, yet admirably introductory, is Ernest Weekley's *The English Language* (Andre Deutsch); for those requiring more about American English and much more about the Indo-European languages, Eric Partridge's *The World of Words* (Hamish Hamilton) is suggested. All four books can be read with ease by even a beginner.

USAGE

The books on usage mentioned in Chapter I are H. W. Fowler's *Modern English Usage* (Oxford University Press) and Eric Partridge's *Usage and Abusage: A Guide to Good English*, recently brought up-to-date, revised and enlarged, and *The Concise Usage and Abusage* (both published by Hamish Hamilton). Various subjects and points belonging to usage form the matter of my *Good English* and *Better English*, which appear as 'paperbacks' in Pan Books and in 'library editions' in the Language Library (Andre Deutsch); the latter editions, more comprehensive than the former, are preferable for students and teachers.

VOCABULARY

The quickest and easiest, but also the safest, way to gain an adequate idea of the vocabulary of English is to browse in a good dictionary. The three best short dictionaries of English are: *The Concise Oxford* (Oxford University Press) for the student and the person with literary tastes; *Chambers's Twentieth Century* (Chambers) for the general purposes of the 'man in the street'; and, combining something of both qualities, D. C. Browning's first-rate *Everyman's* (Dent). Among dictionaries standing midway between these and *The Shorter Oxford*, the best is *The American College* (Random House). Beside *The Shorter Oxford* ranks Wyld's *Universal* (Routledge and Kegan Paul). Larger still is Webster's *New International* (Merriam-Webster; George Bell).

For slang and colloquialisms, only one book needs to be mentioned – Eric Partridge's *Dictionary of Slang and Unconventional English* (Routledge) but it is not for mealy-mouthed Puritans.

FIGURE AND IMAGERY
Sufficiently covered in Chapter III.

QUOTATION AND ALLUSION
There are four very good large dictionaries of quotations: Bartlett's (Macmillan), Benham's (Harrap), *The Oxford Book* (Oxford University Press), Stevenson's (Cassell), of

which the first and the last are American and the last is the most comprehensive; yet even Stevenson's should be supplemented by his *Proverbs, Maxims and Familiar Phrases* (Routledge).

At the head of any list of middle-sized dictionaries I place D. C. Browning's *Everyman's Book* (Dent); note also his *Shakespeare Quotations* (Dent). Then there is also an exciting small dictionary: Eric Partridge's *A First Book*.

SPEECH IN LITERATURE

J. R. Sutherland's *The Oxford Book of English Talk* (Oxford University Press) and Logan Pearsall Smith's *Words and Idioms* (Constable). These two books are, the former edited, the latter written, by masters of their subjects.

RHYTHM IN PROSE AND VERSE

Mr Carey's book on punctuation (referred to on page 159) is published by the Cambridge University Press; Mr Partridge's (referred to on page 159), by Hamish Hamilton.

STYLE

Passim: my *Good English* and *Better English*. 'Style', a chapter in Book III of Eric Partridge's *English: A Course for Human Beings* (Macdonald) – described by this century's greatest authority upon the teaching of English, George Sampson, as 'much the best course of English ever written'.

INDEX

221